Great Careers for People Interested in Film, Video, & Photography

by
David Rising

Trifolium Books Inc.

TORONTO

Weigl Educational Publishers Limited

CALGARY

Trifolium Books Inc.
238 Davenport Road, Suite 28
Toronto, Ontario, Canada M5R 1J6

Weigl Educational Publishers Limited
1900A - 11th St. S.E.
Calgary, Alberta, Canada T2G 3G2

Canadian Cataloguing in Publication Data

Rising, David, 1968-
Great careers for people interested in film, video, & photography

(Career connections)
Includes index.
ISBN 1-895579-22-8

1. Photography — Vocational guidance — Juvenile literature.
2. Motion pictures — Vocational guidance — Juvenile literature.
3. Television —Vocational guidance — Juvenile literature.
I. Title. II. Series: Career connections (Toronto, Ont.).

TR154.R58 1994 j770'.23'2 C94-930767-X

Design concept: Julian Cleva
Design and layout: Warren Clark
Editors: Susan Lawrence, Lynne Missen
Project coordinator, proofreader: Diane Klim
Production coordinator: Amanda Woodrow
Content review: Mary Kay Winter

Printed and bound in Canada
10 9 8 7 6 5 4 3 2 1

This book's text stock contains more than 50% recycled paper.

The activities in this book have been tested and are safe when carried out as suggested. The publishers can accept no responsibility for any damage caused or sustained by use or misuse of ideas or materials mentioned in the activities.

Acknowledgments
The author and the publishers wish to thank those people whose careers are featured in this book for allowing us to interview and photograph them at work. Their love for their chosen careers has made our task an enjoyable one.

The author's thanks go to Heather and Hensley for their support at home, Susan for putting up with the questions of a neophyte, and above all to his mom, for getting him started.

Contents

Featured profiles

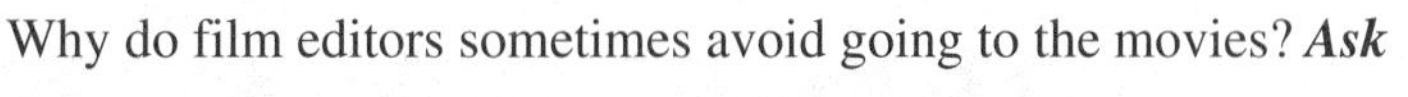

Juliana Chun

Assistant Film Editor

PERSONAL PROFILE

Career: Assistant film editor. "I help keep things organized for the editor."

Interests: "I used to enjoy going to the movies, but it's not much of an escape to go from the editing room to a movie. Now, I wait for my vacation and visit friends in Europe."

Latest accomplishment: "I worked on five film shorts and five music videos recently, and some of them made it into the Atlantic Film Festival."

Why I do what I do: "I enjoy editing and I'm good at it. The pay is decent. And I want to be an editor, so I have to pay my dues."

I am: Personable and outgoing. "My job is actually kind of a contradiction of my personality, since I tend to work alone in a dark room most of the time."

What I wanted to be when I was in school: "A professional musician. I studied cello for 20 years, but I didn't believe I'd be able to play with the best orchestras, so I made a career change."

What an assistant film editor does

When a movie or a commercial is made, each scene is shot a number of different ways. Each shot is different, whether it's because of some change in the lighting, another camera position, or variations in the acting. When shooting is complete, there may be anywhere from 10 to 30 times the footage of the final product. There are literally hundreds of different ways the film could be put together.

This is where the editor's job starts. "Editors have to sort through this massive amount of film," explains Juliana, "and choose which material best reflects the feeling the director is looking for. Then, we have to put that material together to make a good film and meet our deadline.

"The company that I work for specializes in commercials for television," says Juliana. "I help my editor keep lines of communication open with the company's clients (often advertising agencies), and do some cutting. When a commercial is shot, it is done on film. Once that film is developed, a tape operator in our studio transfers it to 3/4-inch videotape, which is working-quality tape. This is good enough for working on, but not for broadcasting. The work we do is mostly off-line editing. Once we've put the commercial together on this kind of tape, we then take it to the advertising agency to see if they like the cuts — in other words, the scenes we've put together. Once we've got all the necessary approvals, and no further changes need to be made, we begin on-line editing."

Playing with color

"In the on-line editing suite, the main thing we do is color-correct the scenes," explains Juliana. "I work with colorists, the people who make color changes. You can ask them to do something as simple as taking out a bit of red or you can ask them to make the flesh tones deeper and the sky more blue. Their range is amazing. Once the scenes are color-corrected, we lay them down onto one-inch videotape, which is broadcast-quality tape. The reason we do it this way is that the cost of an on-line edit suite starts at about $450 per hour. If we did our actual editing there, the client would end up paying a lot more money for the same product."

With a bank of VCRs at her right, Juliana sets up a video for off-line editing.

Editing lingo

Cutting: Putting the films together. Editors used to work with film, which they would actually cut into pieces and splice (join). The technology has changed and most editing is now done on videotape. Editors still refer to their task as "cutting," even though videotape is never cut.

Off-line editing: Editing using less-expensive videotape machines and 3/4-inch videotape to make a rough or working copy. The final off-line version then has to be on-line edited.

On-line editing: Editing using expensive videotape machines, and usually one-inch videotape, to produce a high-quality copy that's ready to be broadcast on television.

Reel: An editor's resumé. When editors used to work with film, they would splice together examples of their best work and put it onto metal film reels. Now, editors' resumés are on videotape, but they're still called "reels."

All in a day's work

A good assistant editor is invaluable. "The idea is for an editor just to cut and leave everything else to the assistant," explains Juliana. "You've got to be really quick — quick working and quick to learn. If you're too slow, everyone gets really impatient. You're given a lot of responsibility. You've got the producers and directors calling asking about the progress of the edit. If you're not right on top of everything, they're not going to talk to you.

"As an assistant editor, I'm often asked to do some cutting myself. But I don't have an assistant to help me, and I'll tell you, it gets really intense. You have to get a job done by a certain set deadline, but people are always interrupting you during the process. In order to keep sane in this business, you really need an assistant you can rely on."

Around the world

Because commercials are so expensive to make, companies may film only one commercial and use the same footage all around the world. Almost always, however, a product is packaged and named differently in other countries. We may know a product by one name in English, but the same product is likely called something entirely different in, say, Germany and Mexico. This presents a special challenge for editors. Once the commercial is done in its original language, product shots must be changed to match the countries where the commercial will air. Sometimes this means creating as many as 15 to 20 different commercials.

It's a rush

"Making a commercial is pretty hectic work because you have to stick to a strict time line," says Juliana. "When a commercial comes in our door, there is already a broadcast date for it. We've got to make sure the commercial is finished by that time, even if we have to work all night to do it. I go to the lab and get the developed film rolls, which are called 'rushes.' The producer and director, who work for the ad agency, come in and look through the rushes just to make sure everything has come out okay, and then they leave. Then, we cut all day and set up a screening for the next day to show them what we've done. Usually it takes only a day for one commercial spot. Often, to save money in filming, companies will shoot a bunch of footage, and want, say, one 30-second and two 60-second commercials from it. If this is the case, we'll get two, maybe three, days to do our work.

Sometimes Juliana's day starts here in the projection room, where she sets up uncut rushes for the editor to view.

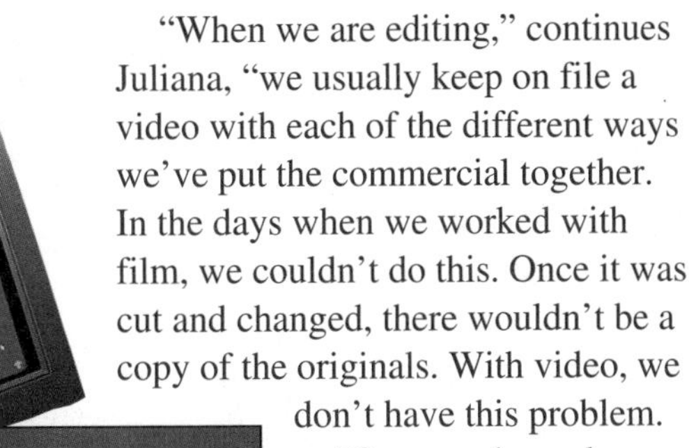

"When we are editing," continues Juliana, "we usually keep on file a video with each of the different ways we've put the commercial together. In the days when we worked with film, we couldn't do this. Once it was cut and changed, there wouldn't be a copy of the originals. With video, we don't have this problem.

"Once we have done several versions of the commercial, the director and producer come to see them. We call this a 'rough-cut screening.'

With computer editing, Juliana doesn't have to scan the entire tape to find the scene she wants; she simply calls up the number of the scene.

This is the first time these people have seen the commercial and they'll usually have a couple of comments like 'Let's use another take because I don't like the way the actor looks here.' Once we change it so they're happy, they bring in their account people to watch it. The account people from the advertising agency represent the company that commissioned the commercial and pays for it. They may make a couple of changes. Finally, we set up a client screening. This is where we get the final approval. If the clients approve — and they usually do — we take the film in for color correction, transfer it to one-inch videotape, and the commercial is done. All of this will have taken place in three or four days."

Activity

Edit your own show

One of the best ways to get a feel for editing is to get some real footage and edit it. Here's a good exercise to do. It involves making a video of scenes from your favorite television program. Remember, the key is to make sure the scenes flow together well.

1. Obtain a VCR and tape several episodes of your favorite program.
2. Look through the footage you've taped and pick out segments from different shows that fit together particularly well. Pick segments with something in common, such as the same character, mood, or location.
3. Hook up your VCR to another VCR or camcorder; you may have to borrow one from a friend or rent one from a video store. Go to the first scene in the first VCR and put a blank tape into the second. At the same time, press the play button on the first VCR and the record button on the second. When you've copied (or dubbed) the first scene onto your blank tape, do the same thing with the other scenes you've chosen.
4. When you're done, play back the tape in the second VCR. If it looks good and the scenes flow well together, congratulations. If it doesn't work well, try to figure out why.
5. Watch the tape with some friends and ask for feedback from them. Do the scenes fit well together? Are there some that are too much the same? How could you improve the tape?

Before editing begins, a tape operator must transfer many reels of film to videotape.

How to become an assistant film editor

If you're looking for a job as an assistant editor, you generally send employers a reel, showing them some samples of your editing. Juliana's studio receives lots of reels. When editors review these resumés, they're looking for what people have done, how they've done it, and what it looks like.

"Now, in order to have work to put on your reel, you've got to be already working," says Juliana. "It seems like an impossible mission, but it really isn't. The best place to do the kind of work you want to put on a reel is in school. Of course, after you've done professional work, you'll replace these vignettes, but it's a good way to start. We have a guy at our studio right now who's doing an internship through a college program. I think he'll be really good. He's learning things with us and actually cutting stuff at school where they have equipment he can use. Granted, the school doesn't have as high-quality equipment as we do, but if you can run the equipment at school, you should be able to catch on in the real world quickly. But you've got to do the work in school. You've got to be cutting a lot in order to have any kind of a reel to send out. When I was in film school, I was working as many hours as I am now. That's the kind of commitment it takes to build up a good enough reel to get a job."

How video has changed an editor's job

Juliana got her first job in the field as an assistant editor in Chicago eight years ago. At that time, most editing was done on film rather than on video. "When we'd work on a film, we'd literally cut the different frames out," explains Juliana. "There would be little bits and pieces everywhere. As a beginning assistant, I was personally accountable for every single frame. I'd have to find a frame for the editor at a moment's notice so as not to hold up the production. It was pretty frightening at times, but taught me organizational skills that have come in really handy."

Now that most editing is done with video rather than film, these flatbeds, which are used for cutting film, are almost as outdated as typewriters. However, just a few years ago, they were a film editor's main tool.

Is this career for you?

Although Juliana sometimes works a 40-hour week, she more often puts in between 60 and 100 hours a week. That's 10 to 17 hours a day, six days a week. "If you're interested in becoming an assistant editor, you'd better be prepared to work long hours," Juliana advises. "I love my work so I don't mind the hours, but many people don't make it. For example, last March and April, there was an advertising war going on between two of the biggest breweries and one of them was our client. It was nuts! As they were shooting their commercials, we were cutting. The whole process, from filming to the final product, took just over three days. I didn't sleep at all during that time. But we beat the other company and got our commercial out first. That's what counts in this business."

"I never thought I'd be working on commercials," says Juliana. "I'm still hoping to work on a television series or a movie, if possible.

Commercials or film?

Many people, like the editor I work for, love working on commercials because they're simple and quick. As he says, 'Think of working on a bad commercial. Then think of working on that bad commercial for six months!' In commercial work, if the material is bad, the pain is relatively brief, but if you're working on a bad movie, it goes on for a long time. Still, I'd rather do movie work. In the long run, it's more rewarding. Good movies can move people, make them think, affect their lives. Commercials just aren't the same."

However, commercials provide more regular employment than movies and are good training. That is why Juliana works where she does.

Career planning

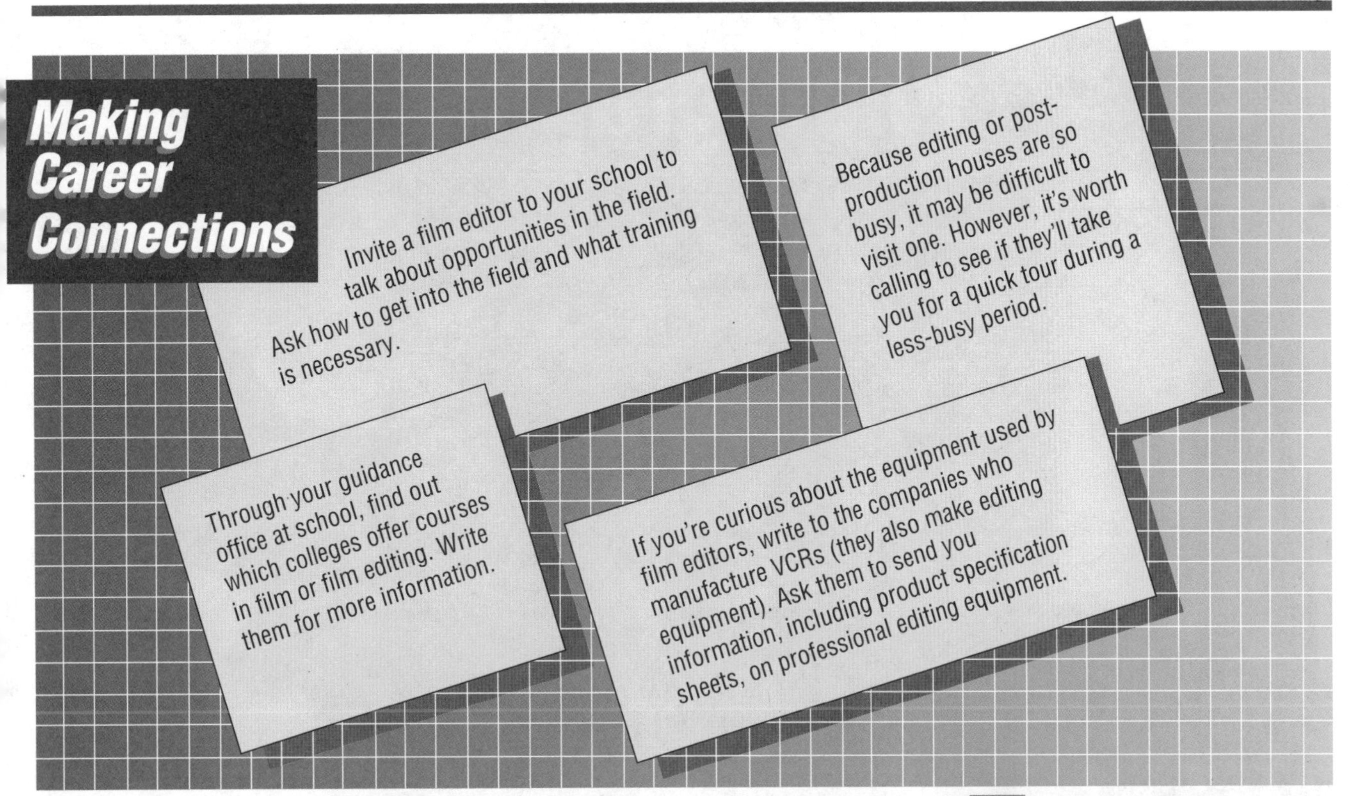

Getting started

Interested in becoming an assistant editor? Here's what you can do now.

1. Learn as much as you can about video technology. Use the editing features on a camcorder to make a short film. Experiment with whatever effects the camcorder has, such as titles, superimposed images, fade-in, and fade-out.
2. Read video magazines and computer magazines to keep up to date on the latest technology that's available.
3. Learn how to edit a good home video. Instructional videos, available at local libraries, always have segments on how to edit.
4. Analyze films, television shows, and commercials while you watch them. Instead of paying attention to the plot, turn the sound off and pay attention to the visuals. Think about why the editor made certain cuts and what you might do differently.

Related careers

Here are some related careers you may want to check out.

Tape operator
Loads, labels, and records tapes and transfers film to videotape. On the way to becoming an editor, many people start as a tape operator.

Colorist
Works with an editor and uses machines in a color-correction suite to change colors, often enhancing skin tones or brightening images.

Voiceover
Adds the voice to commercials when a narrator is needed. Also creates voices for cartoon characters and inanimate objects when necessary.

Sound designer
Adds sound to a commercial or film, hiring musicians to write the music, and putting in voiceovers and sound effects.

Future watch

The field of film editing is changing quickly. Juliana, who learned to work with film just eight years ago, now works on video. In addition, she's learning a still newer system — computer editing — where films are read into a computer and stored on a hard drive. As the prices of these computer systems become lower, editors may be able to do off-line editing on their own at home.

Keith Penner

Photographer

KEITH PENNER
PHOTOGRAPHY
LERY

PERSONAL PROFILE

Career: Photographer. "I'm basically a general practitioner of photography. I do everything from product photography to models' portfolio shots."

Interests: Photography and music. "I used to be the drummer in a band that toured the country, but I got tired of eating macaroni and cheese and living on $30 a week."

Latest accomplishment: "I was recently named the official photographer for *Actors' Equity News*. I'm working on a number of portraits for them."

Why I do what I do: "Something has to pay the bills! Just kidding — I love it and I'm thankful I'm making a living doing something I love."

I am: Inclined to hang out with the freakiest photographers.

What I wanted to be when I was in school: "I kept sane in high school by playing the drums. In my second year, I got involved in photography."

What a photographer does

The world would be a drab place without the work of professional photographers. Everywhere you look you see examples of their work — whether in the morning newspaper, magazine ads, or a wedding album. Photography is a hobby for many people, but it's a different matter when you make your living at it, as Keith Penner does.

"Although I specialize in black-and-white portraits," says Keith, "I really have to do a bit of everything. In this business you have to find an area you can focus on, develop, and do well in, so you can build a customer base. If you get repeat customers, you can spend less time actively seeking clients. Then, you can have more time to pursue artistic photography. Artistic photography is the most interesting to me, but it doesn't bring in much money."

Finding clients

"There are three ways in which I get my clients," Keith explains. "I have an ongoing relationship with modeling agencies. They send me models to photograph, I have walk-in business off the street, and I have referrals. All are important, but in different ways. The agencies send me a lot of business, but don't pay very well. Usually if an agency sends me someone, then that person pays the wholesale rate — just above my costs. I can charge full price to people off the street for their portfolio shots, whereas if they're sent by an agency, they might pay less than half that. I have to charge less for agencies, because they're a good source of business.

"Word-of-mouth referrals are the best clients for me. They come because they, or people they know, were impressed by my work, but I can still charge them full rates."

Different styles

All photographers have their own distinctive style. In fact, distinctive style is what people pay for when they have their shots taken. "I've had some beginning models approach me and ask how much it would cost to have their portfolio shots taken. When I explain to them that a portfolio is made up of a number of different shoots, they sometimes ask if I can do them all. I say no." Keith laughs, "I mean, it would be great for me to have the income from ten shoots of each model who came to me but it wouldn't be right. They have to have variety in their portfolios, and they have to go to a number of different photographers to get that variety. At my studio, for example, we don't have a lot of props. What we try to work with is lighting and design. I try to keep it simple so that you're more inclined to look at the person than the gimmicks. I also don't like putting people through the paces of being something that they're not. I prefer to be more realistic."

Instead of using props, Keith works with lighting and backgrounds to make his photos of models unique.

All in a week's work

"Some people have a daily routine. Mine is more of a weekly one," Keith remarks. "As with any business, the whole thing with photography is discipline. Before I even think about taking any pictures, I've got to worry about my inventory. I've got to make sure that I don't run out of film in the middle of a shoot. On the other hand, I don't want to have too much money tied up in stock, either. I usually keep an extra hundred feet of film on hand at any given time." Keith buys his film in bulk, by the foot, rather than in the reels that are sold in stores.

"It's also important to do things within a certain time frame, because people expect it," Keith advises. "That's the irony of being your own boss. You'd think it might give you more freedom, but it doesn't. Instead, it makes you accountable to every single one of your customers. I've got things organized so that the contact prints for anything shot in a given week can be picked up the following Tuesday. Contact prints are tiny prints, the size of the negative, from which a customer chooses the shots to be blown up to full size.

"Sometimes I get rush orders and bend the rules, but for the most part, my week stays the same: on Monday, the studio's closed to the public while we develop film and do contact prints and some printing. Tuesday, I shoot, and if I have students working in the darkroom they continue printing. Wednesday, I help out in the darkroom with printing. Thursday, I shoot again. Friday, we print some more. Saturday and Sunday, I reserve for shooting weddings and family portraits, sometimes in my studio and sometimes at the family's home. It depends on what the client wants. On Monday, we start the cycle again."

One long day

"The other day, one of the agencies told me about a client who needed some product shots done for a postcard and a business card. I talked to the people at the company, which produces bread and flour products. I told them that it would take about four hours of work if they first got it all set up the way they wanted and ready to go. They agreed to this and sent an interior designer over to set up the shot.

The designer arrived with the props — sticks of bread, muffins, that kind of thing — and a piece of burlap for a background, but didn't know what she

The chemistry of photography

If you want to know what chemistry has to do with photography, listen to what happened to Keith. "When I mix the chemicals I need for developing film, I always use distilled water," says Keith. "It's important to have the acid or pH level of the water constantly the same. Once I bought a developer that was supposed to have some special property so that it wouldn't be affected by the type of water used. Because of the product's claim, I mixed it with tap water to save money.

"When I started to use this product to develop film, the negatives began looking really flat and the highlights looked pasty. Not only that, skin tones looked off, and the images were so fuzzy that I couldn't see individual hairs on eyelashes. It looked as though I was shooting through a really cheap lens. As it turned out, there was something in the tap water that set the pH level off, and the developer didn't react the way it was supposed to. Now I use only distilled water, regardless of product claims."

Keith sets up his enlarger for printing. He often uses different-colored filters in the enlarger to provide interesting photographic effects.

wanted to do with it all. She hadn't planned the set up so it took forever. By three o'clock in the afternoon, she'd set up. But then we still had to position all the lights and re-do a lot of the set because it would have looked poor on film. So we didn't get to shoot Polaroids until about eight o'clock in the evening. By the time we'd finished with the Polaroids, it was about ten o'clock and we decided to take a break for dinner.

"Over dinner, we looked at the Polaroids and decided to change a few things. After dinner, we went back to the studio, added an extra light to the backdrop, moved some bread around, and started shooting. It was two o'clock in the morning by the time the designer tore down the set. The company got charged my regular price for that. But it was an 11-hour shoot, not to mention the preparation work that I put in beforehand.

"Later, they called up and complained that they didn't get to keep the negatives! The photographer almost always keeps the negatives or transparencies, unless there is some sort of pre-arranged deal. Your negatives are your pension in this job. The hope is that eventually you'll make some additional money from your images in the future. The life of a professional photographer isn't all taking pictures of beautiful people. It's hard work, but I find it rewarding because there's something tangible at the end of it all."

Activity

Make a scrapbook of a week in your life

If you think you're interested in becoming a photographer, here's an exercise that involves both discipline and fun. You'll need to carry around a camera for a week.

1. Borrow a camera, preferably a single-lens reflex (SLR) rather than a viewfinder type. An SLR is the type most professionals use. Its manual settings are necessary to get the exact photos you want.
2. Buy two rolls of 35 mm black-and-white film (100 or 125 ISO speed and 36 exposures per roll).
3. You're going to make a scrapbook of a week in your life. The fun part is that you get to take pictures of whatever you want. And the disciplined part is that you must choose a schedule before you start — say, one picture every hour for eight hours a day, seven days a week — and follow it faithfully. Whatever your schedule, write it down, and be sure you follow it. As you take pictures, experiment by choosing different shutter speeds and f-stop settings on your camera. (The f-stop setting refers to the size of the opening that lets light into the camera. As a rough rule, you'll want an f-stop of 16 when shooting in bright sunshine and 5.6 when shooting indoors or in deep shade.) Sometimes you'll be taking photos when you don't want to and sometimes you'll run out of ideas of what to shoot. But you'll be training your eyes to see fresh opportunities for photos everywhere.
4. For each photo, record in a notebook the time and date it was taken, who the subject was, and the shutter speed and f-stop setting you used. When you photograph people, you might want to write down quotes from them.
5. If you have access to a darkroom, develop your film and print the pictures. If you don't have use of a darkroom, take your film to any commercial photo finisher.

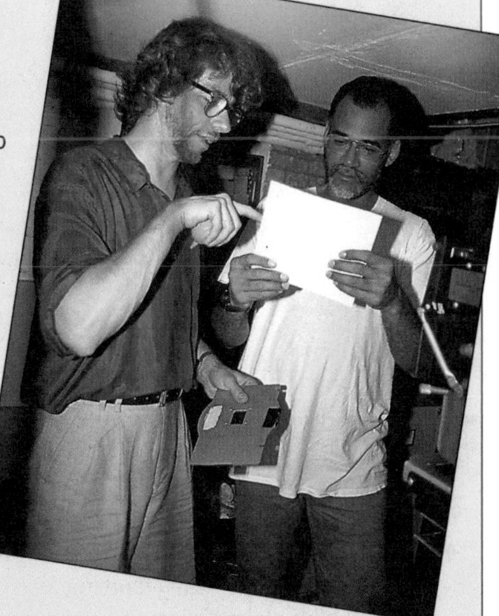

Sometimes Keith likes to get a second opinion on a print before he gives it to a client.

6. Match the photos with your notes about camera settings to see which settings gave pleasing results. Which settings didn't work well? Why? Put your favorite photos into an album, show it to your friends and family, and ask for their comments.

How to become a photographer

"In my second year of high school," Keith recalls, "I had a teacher who used to take pictures of the various bands that played for our dances. One time on a hall bulletin board I spotted a great picture he'd taken of a drummer. He saw me looking at it and asked if I was at all interested in photography. I said I was, and he set me up with a school camera. From there, I started doing shots for the yearbook, and developing and printing my own photos."

After high school, Keith went to college and studied photography. "Before that, photography had just been fun for me," says Keith. "But then it became a grind, and I began thinking 'oh no, I've got to do this assignment learning how to take a photo of a glass.' The more I studied, however, the more I realized how much I had to learn. It was good training for me because it taught me the basics of photography and discipline. It's not the only route you can take, though. I mean, nobody ever comes into the studio and asks to see my diploma. Now, my pictures and my reputation are my credentials.

"An excellent way to learn photography is to do some volunteer work for a photographer in return for knowledge. I'd almost say you'd be better off studying business in school, so that you understand how to run a studio effectively, and then apprenticing with several different photographers. All photographers have their own technique, and you should learn more than one."

Most of Keith's business is model portfolios and promotion shots, like this one of the zany music group called "Trio Mio," done in his studio.

Is this career for you?

In order to be a successful photographer, you have to have an eye for visual detail. Do you notice the wonderful natural lighting that happens in early morning and twilight, and just before and after storms? Can you spot an out-of-focus or blurred picture? Do you recognize when colors are (or aren't) true to life? You've got to have an instinctive eye for that sort of detail, but you can train yourself to be more visual. The best way to do that is to carry your camera everywhere with you and take lots of pictures. Then pick out the ones that work well and try to figure out why.

Keen amateur photographers say that if you get one good photo in a roll of 24, you're doing well. Professionals like Keith will often shoot 100 exposures in order to get one professional portrait.

You also need to learn how to keep track of inventory, do accounts, organize your time, advertise yourself, hire assistants, and run a small business if you want to be a professional photographer.

Samples of Keith's recent work completely cover the wall above his desk.

Career planning

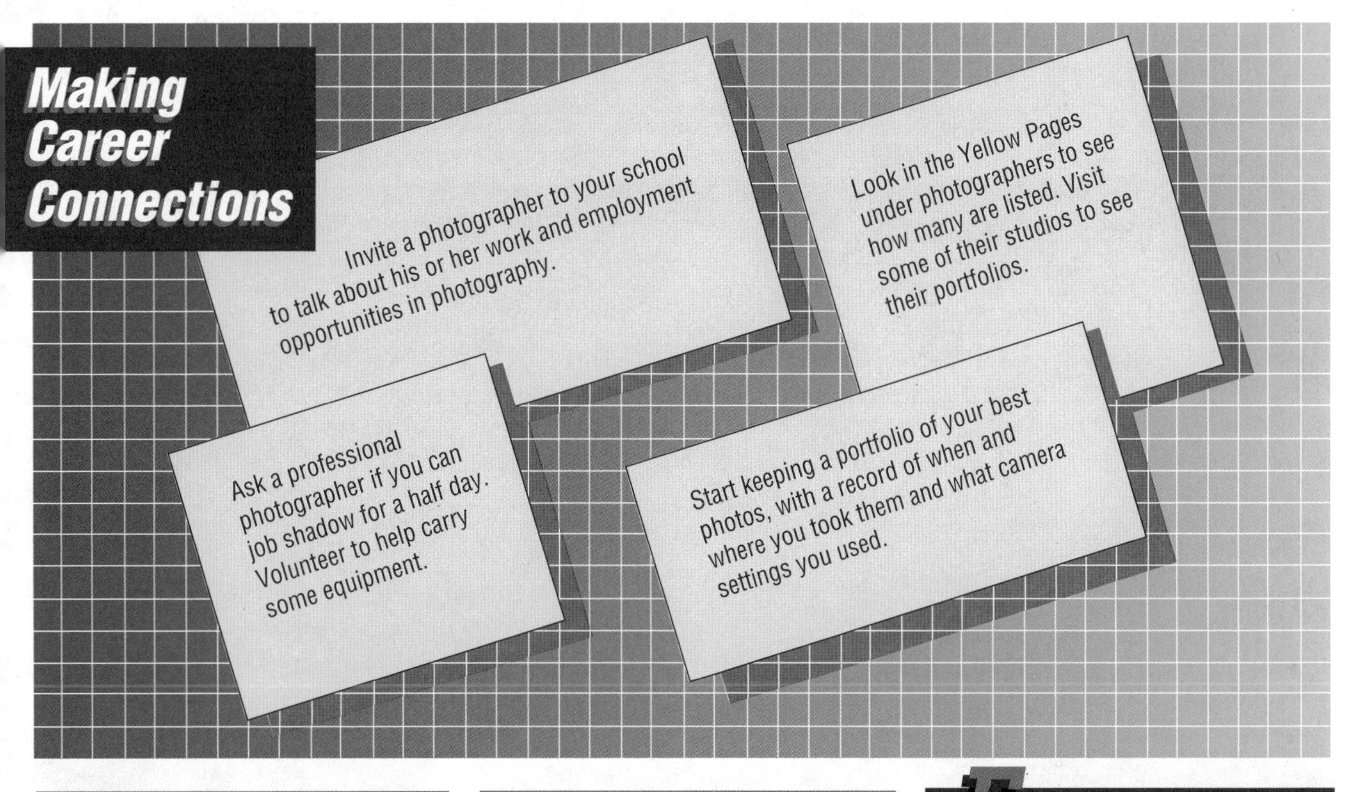

Getting started

Interested in becoming a professional photographer? Here's what you can do now.

1. Work for your school yearbook as a photographer. You can learn a lot by taking hundreds of photos.
2. Ask a professional photographer if you can do some work as a part-time volunteer. It's a valuable way to learn about the ins and outs of photography.
3. Read photo magazines. Notice the credits (the photographers' names, which usually appear in tiny type beside each photo). Keep a list of your favorite photographers. When you are looking for full-time work as a photographer, this list will be a starting point.
4. Visit camera stores to see the many different types of cameras available. If you're planning to buy one, it's a good idea to do research.

Related careers

Here are some related careers you may want to check out.

Photographer's assistant
Helps the photographer develop film, print pictures, and maintain equipment.

Videographer
Works with video cameras to make movies rather than photos, shooting everything from weddings to the evening news.

Props assistant
Gathers a wide variety of props for product or magazine photo shoots, sets them up, and tears them down.

Talent agent
Looks for prospective models to be photographed for advertisements. Is given a percentage of modeling fee as a "finder's fee."

Future watch

Thanks to computers and the way they can be used to doctor images, we can no longer believe our own eyes when it comes to published photos. It's possible, as one well-known magazine did, to publish a computer-altered photograph of the pyramids in Egypt that shows them closer together than they actually are. It's even possible, given computer images, that there will be little need in the future for developing pictures with old-fashioned chemistry. But photographic skills and creativity will always be necessary, whatever tools are used.

Linda Sims

Television Producer

PERSONAL PROFILE

Career: Television producer. "I assign stories, help producers and reporters develop the stories, track progress, and approve the scripts. I also give the final OK before a show goes on the air."

Interests: "When I have time, I play squash and read mystery novels. But usually, I spend my spare time keeping up with current events by reading magazines and watching TV news.

Latest accomplishment: Being promoted to the position of senior producer.

Why I do what I do: "I love watching history happen."

I am: Organized, confident, and cool under pressure.

What I wanted to be when I was in school: "I wanted a job that would satisfy my curiosity and let me keep learning."

What a television producer does

Have you ever thought about how a TV show is put together? Have you ever considered the amount of work involved in producing a half-hour news program? Have you ever wondered who decides what news is reported? If so, you may have the kind of inquisitive mind needed to produce a TV news program.

"In my profession, you don't have to be an expert on everything," says Linda Sims, senior producer of a television business-news program. "You just have to know enough to ask the right questions. That's the key to this job. You're always talking to people about their fields of expertise, so you have to be able to ask intelligent questions."

Not a typical news show

Linda's program, which airs every Sunday night for a half-hour, has been running for eight years. It's not a typical news show. "I produce a business-news program that is not aimed at business people," Linda explains. "We take business issues and make them more understandable. We're proud that people who didn't think they would ever watch a business show, watch us."

It's a pressure cooker

A television producer interacts with many different people, coordinating all of their work into a smoothly running "machine." The pace of television production is usually frantic, and people are expected to work very quickly. "Some people really thrive on the pressure," says Linda. "A lot of the pressure relates to timelines. You're out gathering facts for a story for a specified time and you must get all your footage during that time frame. Back at the studio, you must rush into the edit suite and edit your story by a certain time, because other people also need to use the equipment. You're always working to deadlines in this business. If you don't meet these deadlines, the 'machine' fails. It's my job to keep the machine running, by overseeing schedules and timelines."

Organization is the key

Linda believes that in this type of job, "you've got to be extremely well organized, because you're in charge of the schedules of so many different people." As senior producer, she has to be even more organized than most. "I'm the one who holds everything together. I make sure that when reporters go out to get a story, they're clear about what the story should say, which people to interview, and where to go to do the interviews. Schedules for story assignments are timed backwards from when the show will appear on air. The senior producer helps everyone scramble over any hurdles along the way."

Who does what?

Every story has a producer, who may also be the reporter. A senior producer coordinates the work of several producers. This job involves more management compared to a producer's job. "Being a senior producer is the closest to a 9-to-5 job I've ever had," smiles Linda.

As senior producer, Linda interacts constantly with other people, often by phone. If a reporter's story isn't coming together as it should, for example, it's up to Linda to help solve the problem.

All in a week's work

For Linda and the team of 40 people who work on the business-news program, a typical work week starts Tuesday morning and runs until Sunday. The team must prepare three stories to fill 22 minutes of interesting, exciting, professional air time on Sunday evening. Not surprisingly, Linda finds that "the people who do best here are those who really thrive under pressure. They find deadlines challenging. They like the fact that projects are not openended. Nothing focuses their attention like the thought of eight minutes of dead air time on Sunday night!"

It all starts with the story meeting

At the beginning of the week, Linda calls a story meeting for everyone who is not out of town working on a story — usually 15 to 20 people. First, Linda reviews the previous week's show with her team to try to determine what worked and what didn't. Then comes a brainstorming session to plan upcoming shows.

"Story meetings and the people who participate in them are very important in producing a great show," explains Linda. "These people are always out talking to others and getting fresh ideas. Many of our feature stories emerge from these ideas. For example, someone might say, 'Oh, I was at one of those new warehouses this weekend. Did you know they're offering home improvement courses?' Then someone else will say, 'I don't even shop at supermarkets any more. I buy everything from warehouse stores.' Finally, someone might add, 'I was speaking with a retail analyst on Saturday night. She said that in five years there will be huge numbers of these warehouse stores and that every retail business will be affected.' There's a story! But we didn't walk into the meeting with someone holding that story idea on a piece of paper. Instead, the meeting is an intelligence-gathering operation."

Developing a story

"Once we come up with the idea for a story," continues Linda, "I assign a 'unit' to cover it, and I become the unit's leader, or, point person. A unit usually consists of a researcher, a producer, and a reporter. At any one moment, I supervise some people looking for stories, as well as others who are starting to edit, write, research, or shoot stories. Some stories take three days to do, and some take three months." During the television season, whether spring or fall, the team members are immersed in different stages of production at any given time. "I'm the editorial gatekeeper to whom they can turn if they need help," comments Linda. "I'm also the person to consult to make sure that a story is evolving in the right way."

Coping with stress

"Some people simply hate pressure and break down under it," Linda observes. "You really have to stay cool in this job, because when everything starts going to pot, you have to keep it together. No matter what."

Linda recalls an experience during the early days of the show, when she and her team were operating on a tight budget. "A large Canadian hardware-store chain had just bought a group of new stores in Texas. The chain had sent many of its managers from Canada to run these stores. But

Frequent meetings with co-workers help Linda stay informed of what's happening.

Know your equipment

"A producer must be familiar with all kinds of equipment," says Linda. "Take the camera, for example. I don't need to operate one, but I have to know what it can do. Otherwise, I'd have no idea what to expect from the camera operator. I also have to understand what kind of lighting is necessary, so we don't waste time in places that are so dark that we can't get any shots. Or, if I send a camera operator to the top of a hill to get a shot that's too far away, that's a waste of time, money, and energy. So I've got to know the tools of the trade!

the chain's executives had misjudged the economy and the Texas market, and the stores they'd bought were plagued with problems. The Canadian managers were in revolt. These managers were launching a lawsuit against their own company. Great story! And I was assigned to report it on-air.

"As the managers gathered from across Texas, I flew in. We all converged at the same hotel. One hour before I arrived, the managers' lawyer had told them not to speak to the press. So there I was, having spent thousands of dollars of the network's money, and my story had evaporated before my eyes. After four or five horrific days of needling and making phone calls, I found one manager in Dallas who agreed to an interview. To get to Dallas, I had to drive through heavy rush-hour traffic on Thanksgiving weekend. I located another manager who wouldn't agree to an interview, but he did drive us around and show us the locations of the hardware stores. It was a nightmare, but I brought back a story because I couldn't go home without one. That's the kind of near-disaster you must be able to handle. It can be a struggle trying to get people to do what they don't want to do."

Activity

Writing a news story

Linda compares the storywriting process to a diamond. "At the tip of the diamond," says Linda, "you have an idea for a story. Next, you need to do lots of research. This information-gathering process is like the expanding shape of the diamond. You read articles, you talk to people, you watch other television shows, you learn everything you can about your subject. Then, you must condense your information into a few sentences. This is similar to the tapering shape of the diamond. Finding a lot of information and reducing it to an interesting, understandable, clear, and entertaining story — that's the art of television production."

IDEA — Gathering information → → → LOTS OF INFORMATION — Condensing information → → → STORY

In television production, it's important to condense material into short, concise stories. Here's a good way to practice this type of writing.

1. Choose a newspaper or magazine article that interests you.
2. Read it aloud in front of a mirror while timing how long it takes.
3. Without changing the story's meaning or losing any important facts, condense the story reading to two minutes — no more, no less. This is harder than it sounds (unless you speak very fast, which is an unacceptable television technique).

How to become a television producer

Thinking back to her high school days, Linda believes English was her most useful course, because she learned some of the communication and writing skills required in television production. "To write stories for television, you must understand grammar and syntax, and you must know how to express yourself well," notes Linda.

After high school, Linda studied French, Spanish, and Old English, which had no direct bearing on television, but which helped her immensely. "What you study isn't important," observes Linda. "It's just important that you study something because a postsecondary education teaches you how to think. It trains you to absorb information and make sense of it. You learn how to make yourself understood, both in writing and in speaking, so that you have some control over your career path. Without these skills, people aren't going to notice you, no matter how smart you are."

Whatever education or training you follow, the business of television is a tough one, and you have to make your own breaks. "I began as a production secretary," recalls Linda. "I worked Monday to Friday, and the show was taped every Saturday. For six months, I went in to watch the taping every Saturday because I wanted to find out how they produced the show. I offered to do any kind of running around. If the team needed to photocopy a page of a script, or if they had forgotten something back at the office, I acted as a gopher. I wasn't paid for my time in the studio, but when a research position opened up, I got the job."

Is this career for you?

To be successful in television takes a special kind of person. You must perform well under pressure. You have to be organized, confident, and adaptable. "This job is the opposite of routine because it is so reactive to world events," notes Linda. "You might arrive at work one morning expecting a calm day, and then, by ten o'clock, be on a plane to London or Los Angeles. Or you could spend the day tramping through a construction site trying to get good shots for a story. On the other hand, you might spend a 16-hour day in the edit suite, because you've got to get the story to air that same week. For people who truly enjoy television production, the fact that anything can happen is the real fun. This industry is definitely good for people who have a low tolerance for boredom!"

Climbing the ladder

If you're interested in television as a career, be prepared to work your way up the ladder. "I started as a secretary and became a researcher," says Linda. "From there, I became a producer for my current show, then an on-air reporter, and now, finally, the show's senior producer. While I'm less involved now in producing individual stories, I would not have this job today without years of production experience behind me."

Once a decision is made about a story, team members must be ready to dash off at short notice. These two recently found themselves in the fashion district of New York city.

Career planning

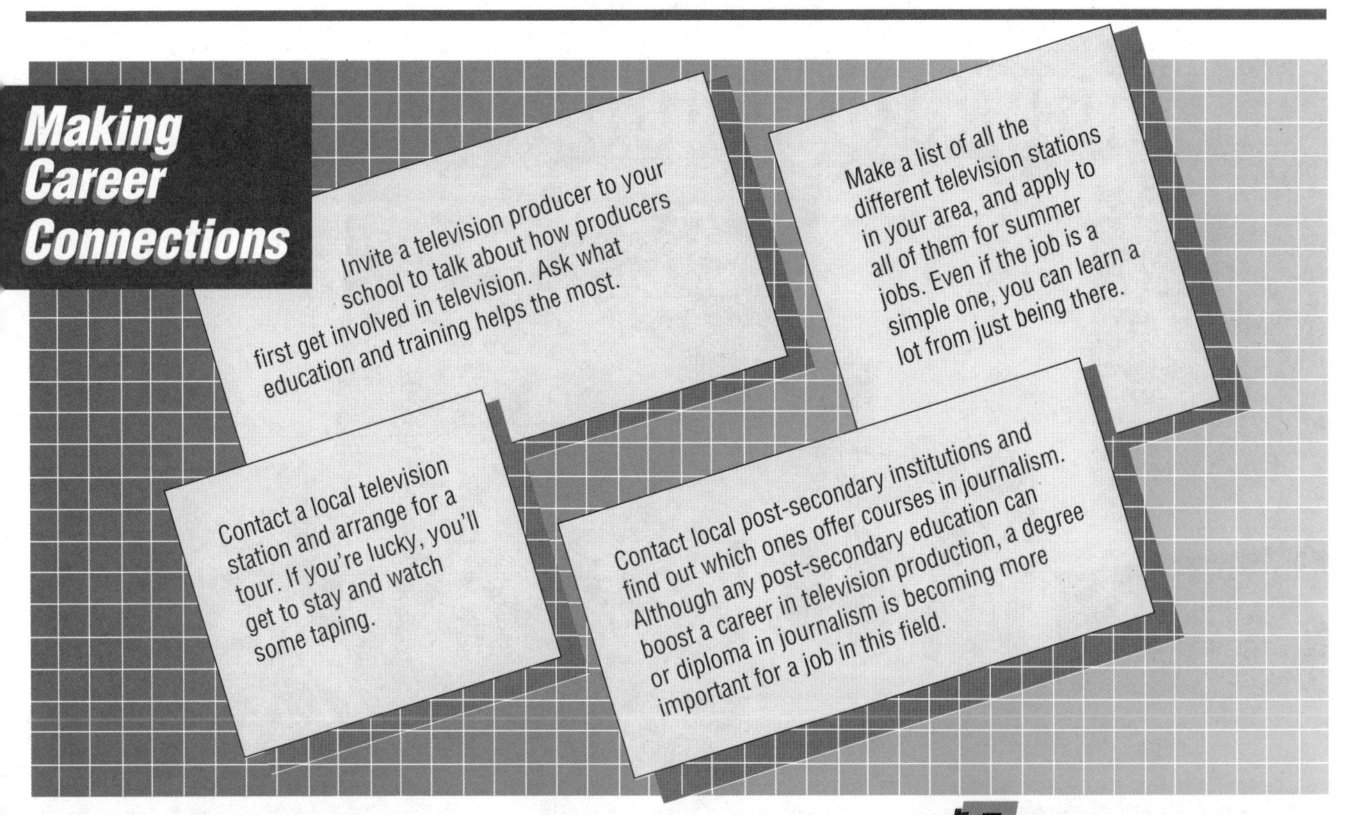

Getting started

Interested in being a television producer? Here's what you can do now.

1. Take English, history, and as many other courses as possible. To work as a television producer, you must be able to communicate well, and both written and verbal presentations are excellent practice for this.
2. Read as many magazines, books, and newspapers as you can. If you want to be in television news, you must keep up-to-date on current events.
3. Watch the television news each day, and compare presentations on different networks. Each show has its own style, which is shaped by the producer. Discuss with your friends which styles you like best.
4. If you can, learn how to use a video camera, and interview a subject or make a mini-documentary as part of a school research project.

Related careers

Here are some related careers you may want to check out.

Researcher
Investigates and gathers information, using the telephone and various resources, such as libraries. Reports findings to a producer.

Reporter
Receives a story assignment, goes on location, gathers additional information about the story, compiles the information, and reports findings in a newscast.

Editor
Condenses filmed material so that it's interesting, exciting, and suited to the time frame specified by the producer.

Future watch

Television is a booming industry. Every year, as technology advances, new innovations appear. Increasingly sophisticated satellite technology could create a global audience for every program. To keep on top of these innovations, motivated and dynamic producers are going to be in great demand in this industry. Given the rapid pace of technological change, the vision and guidance of competent producers will be needed more than ever.

Rion Gonzales

Cinematographer/Director

PERSONAL PROFILE

Career: Cinematographer-director. “On some projects I work as the director, and on others I’m the cinematographer. When I direct, I work more closely with the actors and when I shoot, I work more with the equipment.”

Interests: “I love to experiment with still photography.”

Latest accomplishment: “I just finished shooting a 30-minute documentary about nuclear power plants, and it’s getting very favorable newspaper reviews.”

Why I do what I do: “I love it. The opportunity to dream up something and then bring it to life is totally satisfying to me.”

I am: Personable, creative, and hard working.

What I wanted to be when I was in school: “I really had no idea. It wasn’t until three years after finishing high school that I realized I wanted to work in film. Until then, I’d been working on a degree in chemical engineering. It was a big switch.”

What a cinematographer-director does

On every film set, you'll find a cinematographer (called the director of photography in movie credits) and a director. The two jobs are closely related, and Rion can do both. The director is the person who controls how the script is translated into a film. In other words, the director decides how the scene should look and makes sure the actors are playing their characters convincingly.

The cinematographer is the person who decides how a scene is to be shot. Rion explains: "Let's say the script calls for a shot of someone falling from a bridge — then the cinematographer's job is to make that shot look good. To do this, the cinematographer has to choose where to shoot the scene, in a studio or on location. Cinematographers also have to decide what time of day to shoot, what angles to shoot from, how many cameras to use, what speed of film to use, and what kind of lighting is needed."

Working different jobs

Having a wide range of experience in film production is a big advantage in the industry. "When you get to be a big name like Steven Spielberg, then you may be able to work exclusively as a director," Rion comments. "Otherwise, you usually have to work in other areas as well." In fact, most successful directors have worked in many different jobs along the way. "It's a confusing industry," says Rion. "You can never say 'this is my job, this is what I do.' Your job always crosses over into others. But it's good to know all the different aspects of film production, because they complement each other. As a director, it helps that I know how the cameras operate. It saves everybody time and gives me more respect on the set.

"If I call for a shot, and somebody says that it can't be done but I know it can, we work it out and get that shot. On the other hand, working as a cinematographer, I've been with some directors who had no clue how the equipment operated. They may have had great ideas, but without the practical knowledge of how the equipment works, they couldn't effectively translate that vision to film."

A different kind of film

The last film Rion directed was one that most people will never see. "It was a ten-minute promotional film for a spy thriller," says Rion. "It's not the kind of thing you see before a feature at the movies. It's what we show to different producers in order to raise money. Our producer takes this film short around to other producers and industry people and tries to generate interest in the final film. If there's enough interest and funding, we get to make the feature."

Before shooting, the cinematographer or first assistant always checks the camera to make sure focus settings are correct.

All in a day's work

"Whether I'm hired as a cinematographer or as a director, I'm hired for my style, my coaching ability, my direction, and my sensibility," explains Rion. If Rion is hired as a director, he's responsible for much more than he is when hired as the cinematographer. Once he's awarded a contract for a film, he starts by getting a casting agent to help him find the right actors. After they've chosen the actors, he starts working with them. Together, they go through the script and discuss how Rion wants it to be shot and acted. "This can be the hardest part of the production for the director," Rion remarks.

The art of directing

"When you direct, you have to be prepared for a battle of wills," Rion smiles. "Often the actors feel they know what a character's all about; you have to convince them to act

Lighting creates a dramatic effect on a rock video, for which Rion is the cinematographer. On location shots like these, lights may have to be positioned wherever possible.

The show must go on

Things don't always go as planned in film production, but because of the huge cost involved, the show must go on. Rion recalls one time when the weather wouldn't cooperate. "Last summer, I was shooting a film called *One Summer* up on a northern lake. We were scheduled to be up there for one week, shooting scenes of kids at camp. When we arrived, the temperature dropped to just above freezing, and it started raining. That's how it stayed for the rest of the week. We had to get the shots we needed in that time, so we proceeded. We were all wearing parkas, but on screen the kids had to act like it was summer. When they had to go in the water I felt particularly sorry for them, but we had to either get the shots or scrap the film. They weren't the happiest subjects I've ever worked with," he adds ruefully.

Before shooting a scene, Rion calls for the props person to bring a helmet.

your way. Being a good director doesn't only mean being able to communicate your ideas so that others understand what you want. It also means being able to suggest themselves an idea so that the actors think they came up with it themselves.

Nobody, including actors, really likes being told what to do. But knowing how to handle people is important in the film industry: it's the way to a good production. In order to create your own vision as a director, you plant a seed in the actors' minds and cultivate it. When that seed grows into a tree, they think it's their own, and everybody's happy," Rion laughs. "I hope no actors read this. It might make my job more difficult."

Directing compared with cinematography

In different ways, both the director and the cinematographer greatly affect the final appearance of a film. As Rion describes: "Let's say one of the characters in a film is a psychotic murderer. If I'm the director, I've got to help that actor create background for the character that isn't in the script. Let's say this character becomes violent every time he sees the color red. I may tell the actor, 'The color red makes your blood boil because it reminds you of your uncle who always wore red and who was always yelling at you and your sister when you were young.' The actor will then be able to create his character. But he needs that image so that when he acts like a psychotic murderer, he has something to refer to.

"On the other hand," he continues, "if I were working on the same movie as a cinematographer, I wouldn't work directly with the actors at all. But when it came to shooting the scene, I'd have to make sure that the camera angles and lighting intensify the sinister look of the murderer.

"Directing is a lot of fun and can be very exciting, but I prefer shooting because I tend to be more visual than idea oriented. If you give me an idea, I'll make it look beautiful for you. It's nice to have variety, however, so I think I'll continue with both."

Activity

Make your own movie sequence

As a cinematographer-director you have to be able to work with both the camera and people. Here's a good way to get practice at both.

Look in your local library for a good resource book to show you how to shoot a film sequence (a series of short scenes). Using a camcorder, shoot your own mystery, action, or comedy sequence. Rion has a helpful rule of thumb about how much footage you need: "Professionals tend to shoot at least ten to one. This means that if the final product is supposed to be six minutes long, you should have at least 60 minutes of footage to work with. That way, you edit together all the best shots."

After you've shot your sequence once, see which shots worked and which ones didn't. Are the actors performing the way you think they should? Are the props in the right place? After you've figured out how to shoot it better, go back and try again. Use different lighting and camera angles for better effects.

Most rock videos are shot on 16 mm film, using cameras such as these.

How to become a cinematographer-director

After three years of studying chemical engineering, Rion switched to film studies. There, he learned film theory and different styles of directing. After that, he went to art college, where he learned the practical side of filmmaking: where to position the lights and the camera and how to use the camera effectively.

After graduation, Rion worked in many different jobs. "I started as a P.A. That's a production assistant," he says. "I was kind of a general-purpose 'gopher,' getting anything from coffee to last-minute props. My first day, I worked 22 hours. During a shoot, the P.A. usually works the longest hours. Needless to say, I didn't like it too much," he laughs. "After I had worked as a P.A. for several months, I finally got a job as a grip. The grip is responsible for moving the camera. In other words, if the camera has to get from point A to point B, the grip has to build the mechanical equipment, such as track or scaffolding, to get it there. After working as a grip, I worked as a gaffer (lighting director) for awhile. Then I moved on to be a camera assistant, and from there I moved to where I am now."

Rion and a production assistant assemble the camera dolly — the rolling stand on which the camera sits.

Experience is essential

"Experience is important," declares Rion. "If you're a director or camera operator, you're selling your creative skills, not simply the fact that you know how to operate a camera. In order to sell these skills, you have to show your past experience. To get experience, you have to involve yourself in as many films as possible.

"When I was in film school, I made sure that I worked on other people's productions in different capacities, just to log the hours of work. It's also an advantage to work with as many people as possible, so that your name gets known in film circles. School doesn't really help you get a job, but it teaches you how to use the equipment and guides you in writing and producing. Once you have the educational background, you've got to get out there and use what you've learned to make a name for yourself. The more exposure you get by working on many different productions, the more likely it is that someone will hire you."

Is this career for you?

"Working in the film industry is very hard," says Rion. "When you start out, you work 17- to 22-hour days and are not very well paid. There's not much glamour. I wasn't looking for glamour though. I decided that even if I were a starving filmmaker for the rest of my life, at least when I woke up in the morning, I could smile and feel happy, because I'd be doing what I love. Fortunately, as it worked out, I'm making money too, so I have the best of both worlds."

Try for yourself

Before specializing in film studies, Rion suggests getting a flavor of what film work is like. "If I could have done anything differently," comments Rion, "I would have started a lot earlier. If I were in high school now, I'd start by phoning the local film liaison office to get the numbers for all the productions happening in my area. Then I'd phone the production coordinator for each and ask to work in the camera department for free, to learn the ropes. If you did this, chances are you'd work as a grunt — moving camera equipment from site to site.

Eventually, you'd learn how to fill out the camera report sheets and load and unload the camera. You'd also learn how a production works. And the crew might give you a call and take you on as a trainee at minimum wage for the next production. By doing this, you could learn if you like film work."

Career planning

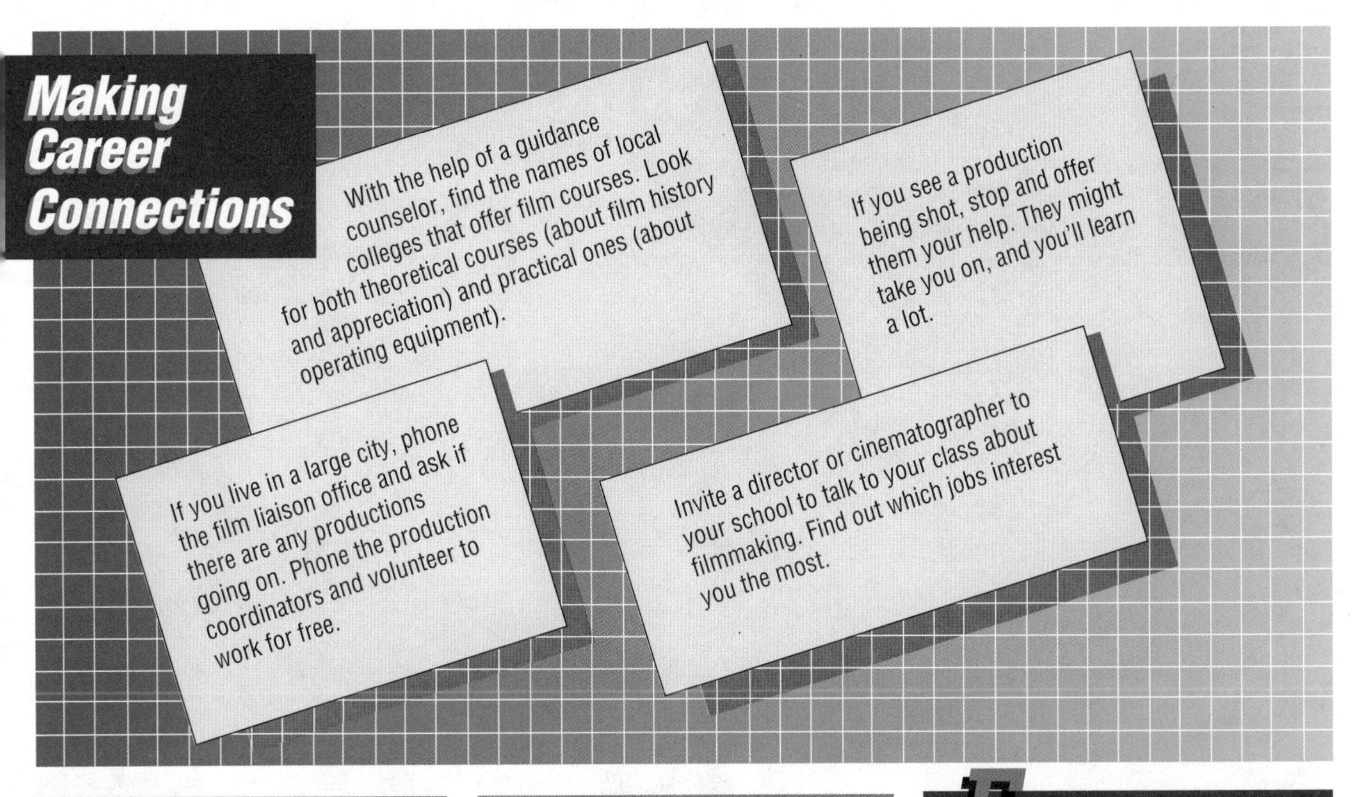

Getting started

Interested in being a cinematographer-director? Here's what you can do now.

1. Take drama in school.
2. Join your school stage crew, where you'll learn about lighting and sound.
3. Try out for the school play as an actor or volunteer as a stagehand. The more exposure you have to acting and working on productions, the easier it will be for you to direct later.
4. Read books on filming and directing and make your own production using a camcorder or an 8 mm movie camera.

Related careers

Here are some related careers you may want to check out.

Gaffer
Heads the lighting department and looks after lighting on the set.

Grip
Builds rigging to move the camera, and scaffolding and special mounts for lighting. Also positions flags, which block and control light and create shadows.

Art director
Heads the art department, which is responsible for designing and building sets and decorating them. Also heavily involved in selecting locations.

Costume designer
Responsible for the costumes for a production, and making sure that they accurately reflect the time period in which the film is set.

Future watch

Ever since motion picture technology began in the early 1900s, the need for directors and cinematographers has been increasing. With the ever-expanding popularity of video, filmmaking is a bigger business than ever. As long as people watch films and television, there will be a need for directors and cinematographers.

Vanessa Vaughan

Film Actor

PERSONAL PROFILE

Career: Film actor. "My career started when I was five years old and I appeared in a documentary about deaf children. Back then, I always looked directly at the camera. I like to think I've progressed a bit."

Interests: Painting, writing, and European movies. "I love foreign films because they're very artistic. Not to mention the subtitles, which help me a lot."

Latest accomplishment: "I just completed playing Mabel Hubbard, the wife of Alexander Graham Bell, in the TV mini-series, *The Sound and the Silence.*"

Why I do what I do: "I believe actors have a responsibility to try to expand people's imaginations."

I am: Creative, spontaneous, flexible, and adventurous. "During a break in shooting my last film, I went bungee jumping into a gorge. It was a great tension-reliever."

What I wanted to be when I was in school: "From a young age, I wanted to be an artist, in all senses of the word. And when I'm not acting, I often paint."

What a film actor does

Most people think acting is the most glamorous job in film production. While this may be true, it's also a hard career to make a living in. To be a good film actor, you have to be able to endure hours, sometimes days, of waiting and then be able to perform instantly and convincingly. Vanessa Vaughan is an actor who plays specialized roles. Because she's deaf, she's able to play the role of a deaf person in a movie better than a hearing person ever could.

Vanessa was first exposed to film at the age of five when she appeared in a documentary on deaf children who were brought up with the auditory/verbal method of learning. This method uses lip-reading and speech rather than sign language. "The first film I made was *Clown White*, when I was nine," says Vanessa. "It was a very intense experience for me. It was so much fun working with all of those people that when it was over, I felt as if there had been a death in my family. I knew I was going to return to acting, but I was young at the time so I didn't pursue it actively.

"Some time later, I sort of fell into another production. Then *Crazy Moon* came along, and I starred in it with Kiefer Sutherland. After that, I decided I'd like to do more work in film and started actively looking for roles."

Although Vanessa always plays characters who are deaf, she prefers to play strong characters whose deafness is not their most important quality. "I loved playing the role of Mabel Hubbard in *The Sound and the Silence*. Bell, as you know, invented the telephone, which paved the way for the hearing aid. I often think that without Bell, we wouldn't have TDDs (telephone devices for the deaf), fax machines, or other modes of communication that are so very important for deaf people. His wife, Mabel, played an instrumental role in his life, encouraging him with his creations and helping him with his experiments."

The business of acting

When actors aren't working, they're usually looking for work. Many actors have to work at other jobs, such as waiting on tables, to make enough money. Vanessa supplements her income from acting by selling her paintings. She explains: "I probably have to look for parts even more than most actors because I can only play very specific characters. When people write scripts they don't necessarily think to write in a role that I could do, so I'm trying to break barriers and change people's minds. Once I showed up at an audition where they were looking for a 40-year-old hearing woman. They weren't expecting someone like me to come to the audition. But I must have triggered a light in their minds, because I got the part even though they had to modify the script a bit."

Recently, many films have been shot in Canada, Eastern Europe, and New Zealand to avoid the higher cost of making a picture in the United States. In fact, shooting in New Zealand has become particularly popular because, according to Vanessa, "it's a small country, but it has such a variety of land. Mountains, tropics, and glaciers are all very close together. For *The Sound and the Silence*, we shot sequences there that were set in Scotland, the United States, and Canada. Of course, shooting every-thing in one place is a lot easier than traipsing from country to country."

When actors are working on location, they often live in trailers such as these.

All in a day's work

"There really is no typical workday for me," Vanessa comments. "When I'm working on a film, it's very intense. Sometimes I have to get up at four or five in the morning and work 16- to 17-hour days. During those periods, my life is just work. When I get home, I have to unwind. After a shoot, I like to spend time alone, usually painting. If you're creative, you have to look inward, so I do a lot of that."

On a shoot

"When I'm on a shoot, there may be something of a routine," explains Vanessa. "The night before, the assistant director will phone me and tell me what my call time is — when I have to show up on set. Usually, though, I'll arrive a couple of hours before I have to perform, so my hair, makeup, and wardrobe can be done in plenty of time. The extra time also gives me a chance to speak with the director about what kind of a feel he or she is looking for in those scenes. It's nice to be able to go over that beforehand with directors, because once filming starts, they have to worry about all kinds of other things like the lighting, the camera, the sound, and the scenery. After that, you wait. Often it depends on the weather. If it is really cloudy and snowy, but the script calls for sunny weather, you've got to wait for the weather to change. Once when we were shooting, a crane at a nearby construction site was making so much noise that we had to wait for it to finish. There's a lot of delay and it can drive you crazy. You either get out and talk to people or stay in your trailer and study the script."

Vanessa plays a free-spirited, independent young girl named Anne in *Crazy Moon*, an unusual love story in which she starred with Kiefer Sutherland.

It's all about compromise

"Once you finally start shooting, there's a lot of compromise involved," Vanessa smiles. "For example, there might be one take that I think is my best performance, but perhaps the camera operator isn't

Lip-reading across a crowded set

On the set, Vanessa uses a sign language interpreter to keep her informed of everything that's going on around her because she can lip-read only one person at a time. "In my early years," she explains, "I didn't have an interpreter because there weren't that many available, and I just didn't think about having one. The director loved it because he was the only person I paid attention to. It didn't matter how noisy it was, I could still lip-read him. Furthermore, he could mouth words to me and nobody else would know what he was telling me, so we could have our own little conversation from across the room."

Powerful lights, shining into an apartment where filming is happening, can make a dull day appear sunny.

happy with the angle it's shot from. So we have to shoot it again. Then, the lighting people might think there's too much glare or too much shadow. So we have to shoot it again. And so on. In the end, it's up to the director and the editor to pick what they think is best."

Sometimes, you also have to compromise with the weather, too. Vanessa recalls one such time. "For the movie *Crazy Moon*, I had to do a number of pool scenes. They were filmed in an outdoor pool that was freezing cold. But there I was in my bathing suit pretending it was sunny and warm. The director was in a wetsuit. The film crew were also in wetsuits. I wanted a wetsuit, too. But once the director said 'action,' I had to block out the cold. Somewhat miraculously, I made it believable that I was warm and enjoying myself."

Give and take

"When I was working on *The Sound and the Silence*, the costume designer wanted us to wear genuine clothing from that historical period," Vanessa recalls. "So the female actors all had to wear tight corsets. We experienced how women must have carried themselves back then, but the corsets were really uncomfortable. While we were complaining about the corsets, the male actors were complaining about having to wear fake beards, which apparently itched. So, a few of the other actors and I got together and asked the director to wear a corset and a fake beard for a day. He looked ridiculous. And from that day on, he understood what we were going through. There is often room for fun on the set."

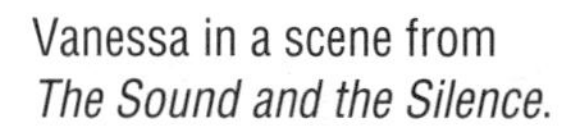

Vanessa in a scene from *The Sound and the Silence.*

Activity

Prepare for an audition

When actors go for auditions, they are usually asked to read from a script or recite a script they have memorized. Here are several ways to practice for an audition.

1. Go to a library and check out several plays that look interesting. Pick one, choose a character, and read that character's lines to a mirror. See if you can do this without stumbling, while still showing the emotion and facial expressions called for in the script. This can be harder than it sounds, but remember — practice makes perfect.
2. If you find a script that is particularly interesting or enjoyable, memorize a ten-minute segment of it. Practice saying all the characters' lines in different tones, using different facial expressions. Once you think you've mastered them, add hand and body motions that you think the characters would have.
3. If you have friends interested in acting, get together with them and read scripts. Critically evaluate each other's performance. Listen to suggestions on how to make your character more convincing and try again.
4. Research by watching movies or television to see how different actors play the same character. For example, compare the many movie portrayals of Robin Hood or of Scrooge in *A Christmas Carol.*

All actors need publicity photos to send to casting agents. Called "head shots," the photos are generally 8- x 10-inch, black-and-white prints.

How to become a film actor

In high school, Vanessa took a lot of courses in drama and fine arts. She found that the course that helped her the most in acting was English, because all the reading helped give her a better feel for language. This is important, because when you're an actor, you can't stumble over words in a script.

Vanessa received her degree in fine arts, but believes that any postsecondary education is valuable for an actor. "It helps you relate to other people," says Vanessa. "It also puts you in an environment that is rich with the exchange of ideas, which helps you learn to articulate your own thoughts. Finally, it helps you learn how to work with people, which is really important, because when you're acting, you're always collaborating with others."

If you want to get into acting, be prepared for many disappointments along the way. People may try to discourage you. "It takes courage and you have to follow your dreams," advises Vanessa. "But you can help yourself," she continues. "Take anything creative in school, because for an actor, creativity is essential. Regardless of what role you're playing, you're putting a bit of you into that role. Also, learn whatever skills you can. Don't concentrate only on acting all the time. The more skills you know, the more marketable you are as an actor. One of the reasons I got the lead role in *Crazy Moon* was that they were looking for a good swimmer, and swimming happened to be one of the skills I'd learned along the way."

Is this career for you?

Although acting can be very glamorous, most of the time it's simply hard work. "I don't sit around and wait for things to happen," laughs Vanessa. "I go to a lot of meetings and auditions and am in constant communication with my manager. My manager is the person who sets up most of the auditions for me and the person through whom I'm able to communicate with other people in the industry. Also, my manager has a greater awareness of how the business and the relationships in the business work. It's really important to find a manager that you feel comfortable with, and with whom you have good rapport. After all, your manager is working for you, and you pay him or her a commission (a percentage of your earnings) for the roles you get.

On the set, it can be hard work, too. When you're working 17-hour days, you really have to take care of yourself. Says Vanessa, "It can be a demanding job physically, so you have to keep healthy and get as much sleep as possible. When I'm not acting or sleeping, I'm studying the script. You have to have the script memorized before you start production, but you are always reviewing it anyway, just to be sure of the fine details. There's really not much leisure time when you're shooting a film."

Under the watchful eye of a leftover mannequin prop from the movie *Crazy Moon*, Vanessa studies a script for an upcoming movie.

Career planning

Getting started

Interested in becoming a film actor? Here's what you can do now.

1. Take drama and English courses in school. Also, don't forget other creative courses such as art and music.
2. Take part in a school play. There is nothing like standing up in front of your peers and acting to see if this is a career for you or not.
3. Watch movies and television critically. Focus on a certain type of character and see how different actors play that character. Copy what you like and discard what you don't.
4. If you have a favorite movie, get the script from it (these can usually be ordered from bookstores). Watch the movie with the volume turned off and read along with the script. Tape yourself to hear how you sound.

Related careers

Here are some related careers you may want to check out.

Stage actor
Acts in live performances (rather than television shows or movies). Has to be able to act to an audience rather than to a camera.

Director
Directs movies, television shows, or commercials. Has to have a good knowledge of both acting and filming and has to be creative — it's the director's guidance that creates the final image.

Wardrobe person
Fits, sews, and presses costumes for actors. May also research and design costumes.

Stunt person
Stands in for the actor when a stunt is performed in a movie production. Has to be in good physical shape, and have professional training.

Future watch

Movies and television will continue to be a popular form of entertainment. With the ever-increasing amount of home movie rentals, there will likely be more movies produced. With more productions, there will be a continuing need for actors. Acting is an ancient profession that never seems to lose popularity.

Takeshi Yano

Multimedia Designer

PERSONAL PROFILE

Career: Multimedia designer.

Interests: "I get the overwhelming urge to build with Lego every now and then."

Latest accomplishment: Designed a demonstration program for a product called "Data Chisel." This is a piece of computer hardware artists can use for scanning sculptures into computers. "My presentation ultimately helped sell Data Chisel to many retailers."

Why I do what I do: "I've been playing with computers since 1979. I think they have a long way to go before all of their applications in the home and workplace are discovered, and I want to be part of that change."

I am: Organized, motivated, and — more than anything else — a problem solver.

What I wanted to be when I was in school: "I wasn't sure, but I knew that I wanted to get into a profession that combined my interests in art, design, and computers."

What a multimedia designer does

A multimedia designer is basically a computer programmer with artistic skills. If you have seen computer-manipulated images in movies or interactive kiosks like the one in the photo, you have seen the work of a multimedia designer. "There are many different aspects to my job," says Takeshi. "I'm part salesperson, part designer, part videographer (video photographer), part computer analyst, and part sound engineer. It's like being the writer, producer, director, and editor of a movie all in one."

Takeshi specializes in product presentation. "When an individual or a company has a product they want to market, they sometimes hire a multimedia designer like me. They tell me what the product does and to whom they wish to sell it. I design a computer simulation that can express all these ideas," he explains. "The simulation combines audio, video, and text to show the customer what the product does and how it does it."

Why a computer?

"A computer can be used to access information stored on laser disk, videotape, and audiotape. It can also control electronic instruments and print video images. Because all these media can be controlled by one computer, you can set up some great kiosks that are totally self-contained."

How an interactive kiosk works

"To create a kiosk that is unique, interesting, and exciting, you have to combine many different creative elements," explains Takeshi. "For example, if I were working on a kiosk for a car manufacturer, I might design a video screen that presents upbeat written data about a new car, along with a powerful image of it. I might also include background theme music generated on a computer that fits the manu-facturer's advertising campaign. Viewers can touch the screen to see more of the car's features. If a viewer touches the part of the screen that displays the engine, for example, an enlarged, detailed image of the engine would appear, with a description of its specifications (the number of cylinders and so on) and perhaps the sound of it revving. The viewer might then touch the part of the screen where the engine's cylinders are shown, and an image of them would flash onto the screen, and so on. The details can go on almost forever," he laughs.

While waiting for her train, a commuter gets information from an interactive kiosk that's promoting the services of a real-estate company.

All in a day's work

Takeshi, who is self-employed, begins his work at 9:00 a.m. each day. "The first thing I do in the morning is to check my E-mail on my computer and respond to any messages. Then, I go through the different computer networks I'm linked to, to see if there's anything that will be of use to my current projects. I can usually get quite a bit of valuable information from the networks, so I make sure I'm on ones that correspond to the projects I'm working on. I also get together frequently with another multimedia designer I know to share ideas and software."

It all starts with research

Takeshi begins each project by first looking at all the material he can find on the subject to understand clearly the background of what he's dealing with. "For example, suppose I were commissioned to create an interactive kiosk at a baseball stadium to help answer people's questions about the game. I would have to dig up all the baseball history, statistics, and rules I could. By knowing as much as possible about the subject, I can come up with a better idea of how to present it.

"I need to know enough about the topic to be able to explain it to the general public. I usually have to assume they know nothing about it," he explains. "I sometimes find myself in libraries for weeks at a time. As I do research on a topic, I make a lot of sketches about how to present it in a visually exciting way. I'm always getting ideas as I research so it's important that I keep a sketchbook. I need to jot my ideas down because there's no way I'm going to remember everything, and I don't want anything to fall by the wayside. Along the way, I look for connections in order to put all the material together."

Once he has enough information, Takeshi storyboards it, which means he works out on a piece of paper how the presentation is going to flow. Storyboarding is done in filmmaking and in advertising as well as in computer programming. "Then I start writing the computer code, and the pieces slowly begin to come together. More often than not, as I'm writing the program, more questions about the subject pop into my mind, and it's back to the library."

Take a break

"It's always a good idea to leave a project for a while and come back to it later," says Takeshi. "Sometimes I have no idea how to start. I might be sitting there, working on a completely different project, when something clicks in my mind and an idea comes to me. Sometimes the only way to get that click is to set the work aside and come back to it later. You can't spend all your time on the same project and remain creative."

Computer programs such as these — the tools of Takeshi's trade — are designed for computer programmers and make his job much easier.

Equations and images

"When I design a computer program, I'm defining images mathematically," says Takeshi. "By making up different equations, I can define where the image appears on the screen and what it does. The mathematics are perfect. But the computer image is always less exact than the math. That's because a mathematical equation can be taken to as many decimal places as you want, but the computer screen is limited in size."

To show something as simple as a cube rotating on a computer screen, Takeshi needs to understand complicated math. Here's the formula for the rotation of a cube, and what it looks like on the computer.

Activity

Storyboarding an idea

To work as a multimedia designer, you need to imagine different ways of presenting information and then illustrate it with storyboards. This activity takes you through a simplified storyboarding process.

1. Imagine that a company has asked you to create an interactive kiosk to advertise one of its products in a train station. Choose a specific product, such as a car, beverage, cosmetic product, or clothing. Think about what information you want to communicate and how you want to involve the viewer.
2. Then storyboard your idea. You may prefer to sketch all the possible steps, as Takeshi has done in this illustration. Or you may want to use magazines to make an even more colorful storyboard. If you use magazines, cut out words and appealing pictures that relate to your product, choosing from both articles and ads in a variety of magazines. Paste two or three scenes together on a large sheet of bristol board or several sheets of construction paper.
3. Show your storyboard to a friend to find out how well you've communicated your idea.

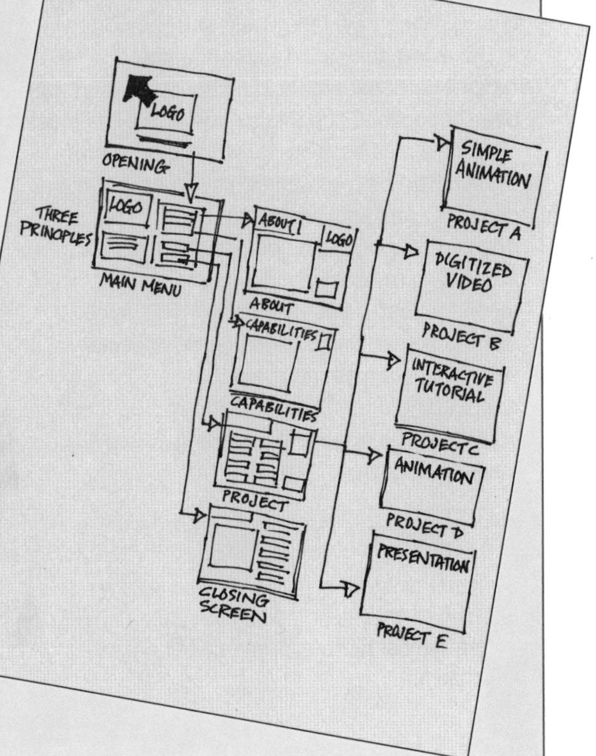

One of Takeshi's rough drawings shows his plans for a brief interactive video that highlights five projects of a client's.

How to become a multimedia designer

"To work as a multimedia designer, you really have to know a bit about a lot and a lot about a bit," explains Takeshi. A strong background in math and computer science is essential. On the other hand, solid artistic skills are needed, too. "It's also important to have good communication skills, which can be developed through courses such as English and history. These courses also teach you research skills, so that you know where to go when you need to get information."

Takeshi's route to multimedia design, however, was a little different from the now-typical path of studying computer science. "When I was in high school, there were no jobs in this field. Careers that combined art and math seemed nonexistent. Following high school, I went to a college that specialized in art. There, I learned more of the practical hands-on side of design and computer programming, but not a lot about research. I learned how to make programs work, but perhaps not the easiest or best methods. I was fairly comfortable with computers already, though, so I was able to learn the best ways of computer programming on my own through trial and error."

Is this career for you?

In addition to having excellent computer programming skills, multimedia designers must also be able to adapt to the project they're working on. "Sometimes, I have to work closely with others on collaborative projects," Takeshi comments. "Other times, I spend literally weeks working alone. It all depends on the nature of the project. That's another reason why I love multimedia design — the variety."

Jack of all trades

"Actually, I call myself Tak of all trades," Takeshi laughs. "One day, I may be a salesperson trying to get a company to hire me for a job. The next day, I'll be a researcher in a library looking through piles of books. Once that's done, I'll be the artist, drawing sketches of what I want to program. Then, I'll be a programmer, keying codes into a computer and staying up all night to make a deadline. Finally, I'll be back to salesperson, presenting my design to the company that hired me in the first place. In simple terms, if you want to be a multimedia designer, especially a self-employed one, you've got to be willing to adapt at the drop of a hat. If you can do that, you'll have an edge in succeeding in this business."

Computer technology is changing so quickly that magazines, rather than books, are Takeshi's most up-to-date source of information.

Career planning

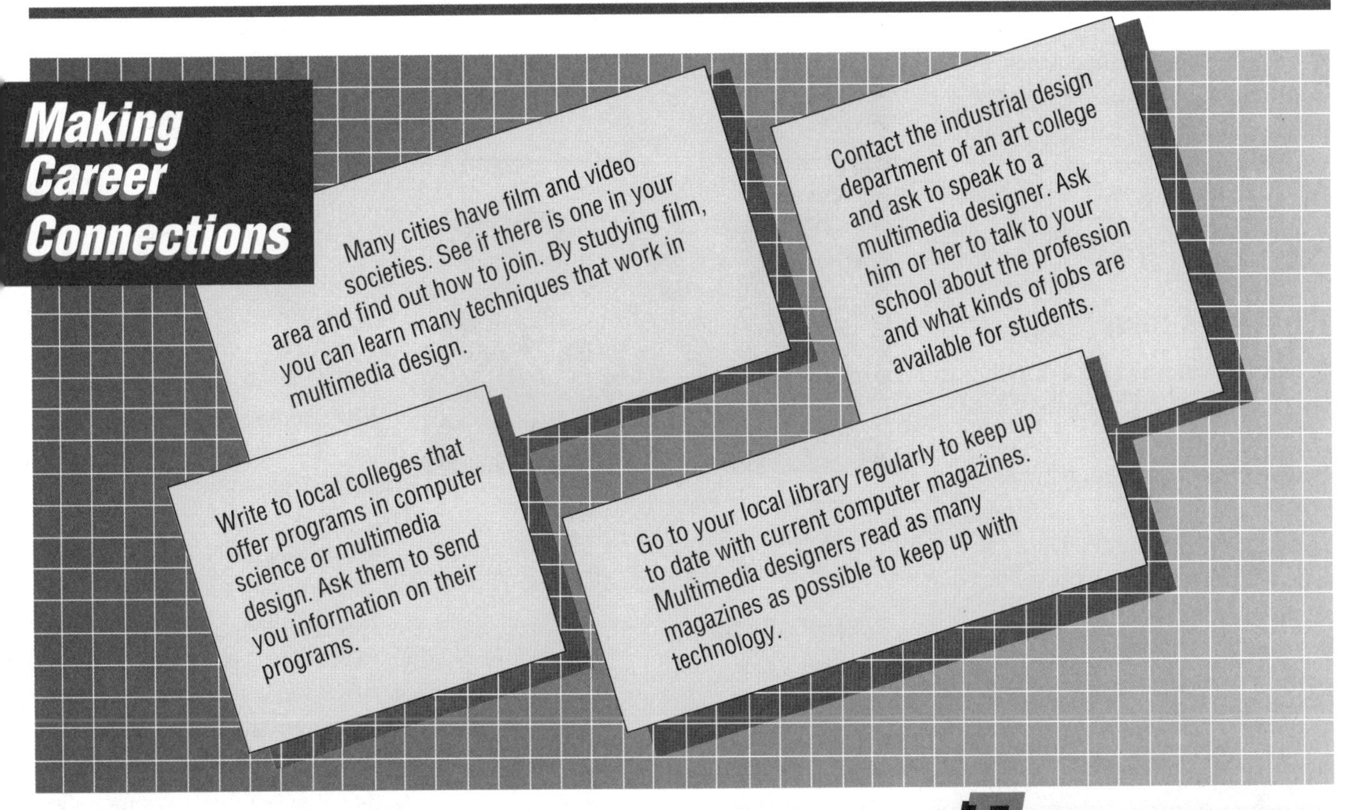

Getting started

Interested in becoming a multimedia designer? Here's what you can do now.

1. Keep your eyes open for video kiosks. You'll be surprised at where you'll find them: in museums, zoos, airports, train stations, hotel lobbies — everywhere! Try them out, experiment with them, and note whether you'd change how they work.
2. Study as much math as possible in school; art, English, science, and computer courses are also helpful.
3. Spend as much time as possible working on a computer. The more you experiment with what a computer can do, the more you'll be able to solve problems later on.
4. Join the staff of your school yearbook so you can learn layout, photography, and copywriting skills.

Related careers

Here are some related careers you may want to check out.

Computer programmer
Writes software for computers, ranging from video games to accounting packages.

Graphic designer
Is responsible for the layout and design of pages in magazines, books, and other print publications. Usually does layout using a computer program, and scans in art.

Videographer
Produces videos, often for teaching, and instructional and business videos that show how to use products.

Artist or Sculptor
May do paintings or sculptures by preference, but usually needs to supplement income by illustrating magazines, books, or advertisements.

Future watch

Career prospects for multimedia designers are very good. The software and equipment they work with are all becoming more accessible and easier to use. Also, the demand for multimedia designers is increasing. "Wherever there is information to communicate, I can help out," Takeshi declares. "And in the future, I think we'll see more and more interactive computer kiosks used in advertising."

Isabelle and Rick Zolkower — Photographic Restorers

If you've ever wished a torn, crumpled, old black-and-white photo could be made like new, then you've wanted the services of Isabelle and Rick Zolkower. They specialize in photographic restoration and retouching.

What gets restored?

"The most common kind of photo we get to restore is the torn, ratty-looking photo that has faded over time. People want the cracks removed and the detail enhanced," explains Isabelle. "We also get a lot of the type of shot where somebody has dug up an old army photo of their dad's platoon, and they want it turned into a portrait of dad alone. We can do all that stuff — and more.

"We work mostly with black-and-white pictures," Isabelle remarks. "Once we've determined how much restoration is needed, we can quote a price and determine how long it will take for us to do."

Rick and Isabelle prefer working at home so they can be close to their children.

The process

"When somebody brings us a photo to work on, Rick makes a copy of it. We never work with the original because if anything happens to it, there's nothing to fall back on.

"Then, the photo comes to me and I fill in what's missing. If I'm fixing a crack across a person's face, I may have to redraw the eyes or nose. If there are unwanted people in the photo, Rick uses an airbrush, which sprays paint in a fine mist, to cover them. Then I'll draw the background in over them. If pieces of the photo are missing, we usually redo the entire background. I usually work with retouching dye applied with a fine paintbrush, and sometimes I use pencil crayons to cover damage.

"Once we've drawn or painted over the damaged parts of the photo, Rick makes a copy of it. Then he reprints it to the size the customer wants."

Combining photos

"When people wanted two or more photographs combined into one, we used to do it by hand, much as I just described," explains Isabelle. "It was really hard to make sure all the people were the same size in the final picture. Rick would spend hours in the darkroom trying to match sizes. Now, we scan the photographs into a computer and do most of the work on them there. Then we take it to a computer service bureau where they make us a negative of the saved image. Finally, Rick prints the negative and the process is complete."

Once a photo is scanned into the computer, Isabelle can enlarge or shrink it or cut off unwanted portions.

Isabelle and Rick can remove from a photo all traces of any distracting background.

Getting started

1. Take art courses in school. A photographic restorer is really an artist and needs excellent painting and sketching skills.
2. Learn black-and-white darkroom skills: developing, enlarging, and printing photos.
3. Learn to use a drawing or painting computer program; it's important to develop computer skills for this job.
4. Try restoring an old black-and-white family photo, working with a copy rather than the original. You can buy dye and pencil crayons at art supply stores and you'll find many helpful tips on picture restoration in photo magazines and books.

Sam Wong — Concert Photographer

Sam Wong makes his living doing what some may consider a dream job: taking pictures of rock musicians at concerts. "It's kind of a fluke that I've made a career out of photographing rock stars," says Sam. "It started out as a hobby. I've always been interested in photography and I worked in a camera store. I also love rock concerts, so I began taking my camera along to concerts for fun.

"Every time I'd get my pictures developed, somebody would want copies. First, I sold 8- x 10-inch photos to friends. Then I started selling them to concert clubs. Because I was at almost every concert, I got to know people in the business, and eventually I was hired by a company that promotes concerts across North America. Once I was hired by them, things got a lot easier for me."

Eventually, he quit his job in the camera store and started taking concert shots full-time. "Now, my company gets me backstage passes for every concert. This way, I don't have to worry about tickets and, since they're the ones producing the concert, I don't have to worry about getting permission to take photos.

The yellow press pass around Sam's neck gives him access to the pit, where photographers shoot from.

"When I go to a concert, I'm usually allowed to take pictures only during the first couple of songs, since performers get distracted by the flash," explains Sam. "With my pass, I have access to the area called the 'pit' — the space between the stage and the fans. Because I'm so close, I'm able to get much better pictures than I used to."

Sam's job now includes being official photographer for two of the local stadiums. "What other job gives you every day off, pays you to go to concerts in the evening and then gives you the best seat in the house to boot?" he asks.

The equipment

"I do all my work with a 35 mm autofocus single-lens reflex camera," says Sam. "There's no way I'd be able to use larger cameras because they take too much time to set up and they're not portable enough." He uses a telephoto zoom lens for intimate closeups and almost always uses film for color prints rather than for slides. "That's because the lighting in concerts is usually so weird, you need to be able to correct it later when printing the photo. With slides, you're pretty much stuck with what you've got. The other reason I use print film is that I've got to be able to develop it quickly — often I have a 2:00 a.m. deadline for the morning paper. If it's a rush job, I usually take the rolls of film to a photo lab with a 45-minute turnaround time."

Newspapers prefer action shots, such as this one Sam took of Paul McCartney when he toured North America recently.

Getting started

1. Join the photography club at school. If there isn't one, why not start one? Ask permission to take pictures of school plays, concerts, and sporting events.
2. Take photography courses in order to improve your skills. Some camera companies offer good short courses in basic photography. If no courses are available in your town, ask at your library about borrowing instructional videos.
3. If you have access to a computer network such as Internet, join a photography news group. Here, you can communicate with camera enthusiasts around the world.
4. Take a lot of photos. There's no substitute for experience.

Shanna Miller — Photo Lab Manager

"When you drop off your film for developing, you usually get several choices as to when you need it back," explains Shanna Miller, manager of a photofinishing store. "Some people think the longer they wait, the better the quality, but that's not true. It takes only about 30 to 40 minutes to develop and print a roll of film, whether you choose one-week or one-hour service. If you want one-hour service, however, you pay more for it." Shanna and her staff have the facilities to process only color-print film at their store; black-and-white film or color slides are sent to head office for processing.

Wearing white gloves to avoid leaving fingerprints, Shanna checks negatives before they go into the print processor.

The process

"There are a number of different steps in developing color-print film," Shanna explains. "First, we have to pull the tip of the film back out of the canister, because most people wind their film all the way in. Then, we splice the film tip onto a plastic card with tracks on it so it can be pulled straight through our negative processing machine. In the processor, the film is developed, fixed, rinsed so that no chemicals remain on it, and dried. This takes between 12 and 15 minutes.

"The next thing I do is look at the negatives to see if there are any obvious problems," Shanna continues. Clear negs or black slides tell her that the film may have been incorrectly loaded so it didn't advance through the camera. Very faint negs or extremely dark slides indicate underexposed film: the flash may have been too weak or too far from the subject or perhaps it wasn't working. She'll mark such problems and return the negatives to the customer, along with a note suggesting what she thinks went wrong.

Then it's onto the printing. Because every brand and speed of film has different properties, Shanna has to set the print processor to different channels for each film type. "If the negs are normal, I can let the machine print on automatic and it will give the best prints possible. Unfortunately, quite often the negs aren't normal, and I have to correct them in the printing," she notes. "It's up to me to correct these photos so they look as good as they can.

"That's really my job as manager: to make sure the machines are clean and running properly and that each print is individually inspected so that customers get the best-quality photos possible. I also make up work schedules for my three employees to ensure there's enough staff at all times, and I handle the accounts."

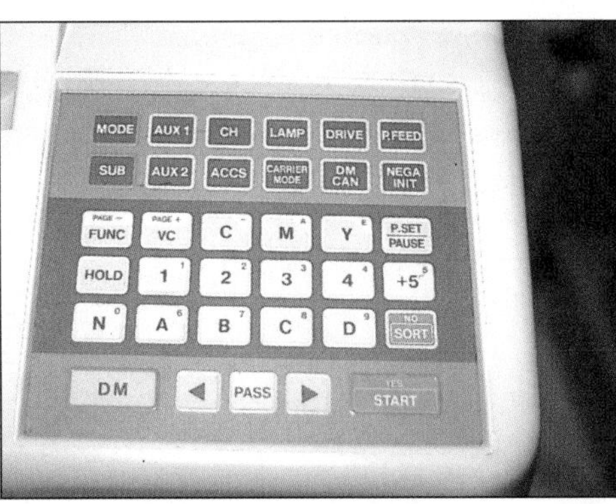

By pressing different buttons on the print processor keypad, Shanna can correct color problems.

Becoming a manager

"When I finished high school, I wasn't sure what career to choose, but I liked working with people, so I got a job in sales at a camera store," says Shanna. "I became more and more interested in the lab and took a company course to learn how to run the equipment. Then I was promoted to assistant manager at a big store that had so many employees and was so busy, I really didn't have time for lab work. Now, I'm the manager of a smaller store, so I get to work both lab and retail — the best of both worlds!"

Getting started

1. Take pictures of something colorful using one particular brand of film. Keeping the lighting exactly the same, change brands of film and take more photos of the same subject. When both films are developed, compare them. Do the reds and blues look different?
2. Visit your local camera store when it's not too busy and ask the manager for a tour of the lab.
3. Keep up to date on film, camera, and processing technology by reading photo magazines.

Brady Gilchrist — Telecommunications Programmer

Brady Gilchrist is the president and C.E.O. of Navtraxx, his own software development company. "Actually," Brady laughs, "I'm more than the Chief Executive Officer, I'm also the O.E.O. or Only Executive Officer." His company produces software for wireless communication.

Because he works with computers, Brady can make his office at home.

"I design software to help in linking computers and communications devices such as pagers," explains Brady. "One piece of software I've developed is called the Electronic Business Card or EBC. "Right now, one of the big trends is that more people are carrying pagers and notebook computers with them everywhere. The EBC is designed to take advantage of this trend. You can now communicate easily with pagers and notebook computers via your computer modem, using an EBC.

"Here's how it works: Instead of giving your clients or potential clients your business card, you give them a computer disk. This disk is your EBC. When your clients get back to the office, all they have to do is put that disk into their computer. A program then automatically boots up, showing on the computer screen the same information a regular business card would have: your name, address, and phone number. An EBC has added features, however. If the clients want to get in touch with you immediately, they just push a computer key to send a message to your paging service. You'll be paged wherever you are. On your pager, the client's number and message (if one was entered) will be displayed."

The EBC also has video and audio options: a picture of yourself and a voice message from you, in case clients want to remind themselves what you look and sound like. "The EBC can also include help files so that your client can call up more information on your company, ordering procedures, customer service support, or whatever else you'd like them to have."

How the EBC opens lines of communication

"The EBC allows your customers to communicate with you wherever you are without having to go through voice mail or secretaries," explains Brady. "Also, it makes it much easier for customers to get the information they need in order to do business. And the easier it is for somebody to do business with you, the more business you're going to get.

"One of the great things about using the EBC is that you can communicate so much more by adding graphics and sound than you can with just text. There's a lot of information you just can't put into writing. Take, for example, a map. Imagine having to put that same amount of information into writing. You couldn't do it. When I develop software, I keep this in mind. I put information into pictures and sound to make it easier for people to understand. The EBC is just one simple example of where this type of communication is going."

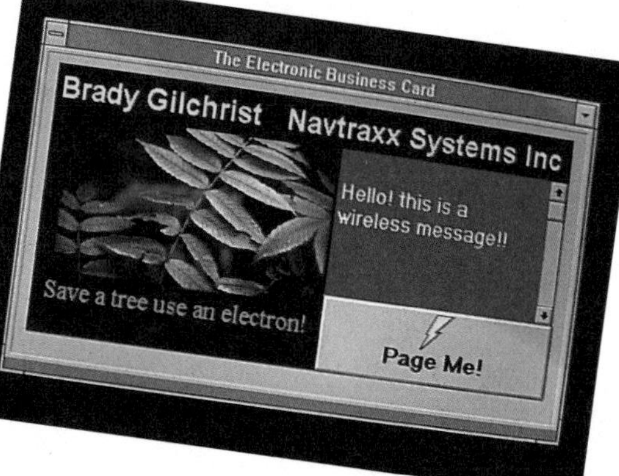

Brady's own electronic business card urges viewers to help save a tree (in other words, not waste paper in a business card) by using his EBC.

Getting started

1. Take computer courses in high school and join a computer club where you can learn about programming.
2. Visit a computer store or phone center and explore the many telecommunications devices available. Can you think of any new uses for these devices?
3. Try to read as many computer magazines as you can get your hands on. That's where you'll be able to find the most up-to-date information on computer innovations.

Classified Advertising

HELP WANTED

EXPANDING BUSINESS NEEDS PARTNERS
Full and part time. You are: ambitious, open-minded determined to SUCCEED. *No capital requirement.* Send resumé or note to: Box 42, 10020 Albert St. Missinabi, Province/State, Postal/Zip code

CANTONESE/ENGLISH BILINGUAL ACCOUNT EXECUTIVE
LEADING telecommunications company is currently expanding in the Oriental communities. Candidate should have at least 2 years sales and marketing experience in this country. Insurance and real estate experience are an asset. $40,000+. QUALIFIED applicant *only*. Please contact R Dept. Manager, Mr. daCosta at 555-0149

CREATIVE WRITER
Wanted for application leading telecommunica nology company. Exp quired. Reply to VR t per. Box 400, The C Keenan Blvd. City, P Postal/Zip Code

Pharmace ical

GRAPHIC ARTIS
Our busy Advertisin epartme and lay out flyers, p ads and
Your related coll diploma i rience that includes iliarity wit QuarkXPress. You w well und priorities and can wo deadlin
Please forward you sumé to: ceuticals Trade 489 Su view Te Zip Code Fax 555-4112 qual op

ACTING INSTRUCTOR
Opeongo College requires a Acting Instructor for the fall/ winter academic year. This is a half-time position for a ten-month contract beginning mid August.
The Instructor will teach both Introductory and Intermediate Acting for 1st and 2nd year students. These courses are University Transfer recognized courses. Possible opportunities to direct College productions exists but is not a job requirement.
Bachelor's degree, acting and directing experience required. Master's degree in a related field preferred.
Deadline for application is June 25. Inquiries can be directed to the Personnel Department
Opeongo College
450 9th Street
Southdown, Province/State

CITY DISPATCHER WANTED
Busy City dispatch requires innovative person to run local truck operation. Require good knowledge of ocean cargo. Apply in confidence to: GENERAL MANAGER P.O. Box 4329, New Amsterdam, Province/State, Postal/Zip Code

SALES REPRESENTATIVE
DUTIES:
Promote and sell h win-dow and d ducts to the home b market in the city.
QUA CATIONS:
• mum three years sales experience in related field
An understanding of the cus-

pe rain. Machin- /Mechanical aptitude an asset. command of English nec Call ABC Wood, Ltd. 555-639 pointment
Please call betw 12 noon.

SCARBIN AND REDVILLE GENERAL HOSPITAL
Registered Nurses
In-patient Services
• Full and Part-time
An active acute care facility, the new In-patient Mental Health Department, will provide the experienced mental health care professional or professionals motivated to pursue career in mental health nursing with an ideal opportunity to broaden their group, interviewing, and counseling skills in a supportive and cooperative setting. The background of the ideal candidate will include recent experience in primary nursing care. General qualifications include a Certificate of Competence from the College of Nurses and

Recre herapist
In co tion with the Occupational Therapist and pr nurses, you will de and implement recreatio s and activit of all types to individual patient ne ssessing nt leisure rests, ions and pla g com- ons are availa As the year of experie in an recognized re tion
nd Redville Ge ls dedicated to invited to apply Resources Office S. Scarbin, Pro

nager
arpenter/Stage
rpentry and ce. In addi- sound. The s and wi
vario rm
by July 9 to: **Ch e ger, on Center for Performin venue ovince/State, Postal/Zip Cod**

PET PORTRAIT PLACE

Photography studio specializing in pet photos requires a receptionist/photographer's assistant. Applicants must be outgoing, friendly, and willing to learn. Previous photographic and/or sales experience an asset. Responsibilities include answering the phone, dealing with customers, cleaning the studio, and doing some darkroom work.

Apply in person, with resumé, to Dina DiMarco, Pet Portrait Place, 365 Lundy's Lane, Springfield. No phone calls, please.

Start Your Own Office Cleaning Business
Be your own boss, the evening anks
For complete information call 555-5190

Weller
JOURNEYMAN MACHINIST
General Machinist, preferably with milling experience required for precision machine shop manufacturing electromechanical sensors. Minimum 5-10 years related experience. Must be capable of reading detailed drawings and working to extremely close tolerances.
No telephone calls please. Forward resumés to:
Mrs. P. Weller
Fred Weller Corporation
34 Leslie Road
Wellington, Province/State
Postal/Zip Code
AWARDS FOR BUSINESS EXCELLENCE

FIRSTLINE HEALTH & RACQUET CLUB
Firstline Health & Racquet Clubs, expanding through Corrale and the surrounding area, offers an exciting and rewarding career in the health & fitness industry. We are currently searching for sales oriented individuals with strong interpersonal skills in the following positions.

1) Membership Consultant
2) Corporate Sales — must have corporate sales experience
3) Program Consultant
4) Cardio Tester

Qualifications:
- Minimum 2 years direct sales experience
- Background in aerobic & anaerobic training
- Knowledge of nutrition

Qualified applicants are invited to call Stan Florry for a confidential interview 555-1305 or fax your resumé to 555-1304

Who got the job?

Finding a job

The first step to success in any career is getting a job. But how do you go about finding one?

- Talk with family, friends, and neighbors and let them know what jobs interest you.

- Respond to "Help Wanted" ads in newspapers.
- Post an advertisement of your skills on a community bulletin board.

- Register at government employment offices or private employment agencies.
- Contact potential employers by phone or in person.
- Send out inquiry letters to companies and follow up with phone calls.

A job application usually consists of a letter and a resumé (a summary of your experience and qualifications for the job). Applicants whose resumés show they are qualified may be invited to a job interview.

Activity

A job in a photography studio

The advertisement shown on the opposite page was placed in a local newspaper. This could be a perfect opportunity for someone who is interested in photography but has little photographic experience.

For an entry-level job like this one, there are likely to be many applicants, but only a few of them will be granted an interview. For this job, the applicants who were interviewed included both Julie Cohen and Matt Leblanc. Their letters and resumés, and the notes made by Dina DiMarco during the interviews, are shown on pages 46 and 47.

Procedure

Read the letters and resumés and make notes about whether each applicant might qualify for the job. Keeping in mind the job description, go through your notes and try to determine which of the two applicants is better suited for the position. In your analysis, consider also Dina DiMarco's notes on the two interviews. What else would you like to know about the applicants? How could their reference materials or performance in the interview have been improved? If you were Dina DiMarco, whom would you hire: Julie or Matt?

Challenge

How would you perform in a job interview? Role-playing can give you practice in asking and in answering questions. Ask a friend to take the role of Dina DiMarco and interview you for the job. Then reverse roles. This practice can help make sure that when you apply for a job, you have a good chance of getting it!

Julie Cohen's application and interview

19 Pine Ridge Road
Springfield, State/Province
Zip/Postal Code

June 14, 19–

Pet Portrait Place
365 Lundy's Lane
Springfield, Province/State
Postal/Zip Code

Re: Advertisement in *The Springfield Times*,
June 13, 19–.

Dear Ms. DiMarco:

I would like to apply for the position of receptionist/photographer's assistant advertised. Enclosed is my resumé, which I hope will interest you.

I have recently graduated from Springfield High School and am interested in a career in photography. While my photographic knowledge is limited, I am a quick learner.

I have worked part-time in various capacities through most of my time in high school. In these jobs, I believe I have learned the communication skills necessary for your position.

Finally, I believe my extracurricular activities prove that I am an outgoing person with excellent people skills.

Please do not hesitate to contact me at 555-4730 for an interview at your convenience.

Sincerely,

Julie Cohen

Julie Cohen

Interview: Julie Cohen

- Showed up early for interview.
- Well groomed, wore attractive clothing.
- Very inquisitive, asked many key questions about how the business works and about how we happened to specialize in animal photos.
- Has a dog and cat, and is familiar with animals.
- Has little knowledge of photography other than using a point-and-shoot camera.
- Kept eye contact for most of interview.

Resumé

Julie Cohen
19 Pine Ridge Road
Springfield, Province/State
Postal/Zip Code
Telephone: 555-4730

Employment

19– - 19–
Part-time salesperson, Dewey-Cheatham stereo store.
Duties included creating displays, customer service, and moving stereo equipment.

19– - 19–
Stockperson, Foodwise grocery store. Part-time. Duties included stocking shelves, cleaning floors, and running cash register.

Education

Graduation Diploma, Springfield High School.

Extracurricular Activities

- Editor, *Springfield High School Yearbook*. Responsible for photo layout and copy editing.
- Head Cheerleader, Springfield High Cheerleading Squad. Responsible for writing/performing new cheers.
- Captain, Springfield High Field Hockey Team. Won championship in 19–, when I was captain.

References

Available on request

Matt Leblanc's application and interview

Interview: Matt Leblanc

- *Very confident and self-assured.*
- *Thinks he knows more about photography than he really does.*
- *Strong handshake and maintained eye contact throughout interview.*
- *Wore jeans and a sweatshirt. Clean, but not terribly professional.*
- *Asked some good questions about what we do here. Enjoys animals.*

1944 Humber Line
Springfield, Province/State
Postal/Zip Code

June 14, 19—

Pet Portrait Place
365 Lundy's Lane
Springfield, State/Province
Zip/Postal Code

Dear Ms. DiMarco:

I read your advertisement for a receptionist/ photographer's assistant in yesterday's paper, and would like to apply for the job.

As you can see from my enclosed resumé, I have a keen interest in photography and believe I would be an asset to your business. I have a good knowledge of 35 mm cameras and have darkroom experience.

In the business I started with my friends, I had to go from door to door to try to find clients and therefore believe I have developed very good interpersonal skills. I welcome challenges and pride myself on my problem-solving abilities. I look forward to an interview.

Yours truly,

Matt Leblanc

Matt Leblanc

Resumé
Matt Leblanc
1944 Humber Line
Springfield, Province/State
Postal/Zip Code
Telephone: 555-4700

Education

19— - 19— Springfield High School

- Graduation Diploma, 19—
- Hockey team 19— - 19—
- Baseball team 19— - 19—
- Yearbook Photographer 19— - 19—
- President of Photography Club 19— - 19—
- Treasurer, Student Council 19—

Work Experience

19— - present

Self-employed. Started my own business with two partners in 19—. In summer, we mow lawns and prune trees. In winter, we shovel snow. Have also raked leaves and walked dogs.

Hobbies

- Photography
- Reading
- Skiing
- Travel

References

Available on request

Index

Credits

(l = left; r = right; t = top; b = bottom; c = center; bl = bottom left; br = bottom right)

All photographs by David Rising, except 14(t) Keith Penner; 20 Citytv 24(b) Suzanne Rimac; 31(b) Jean Marc Derochers; 41(t) Valerie Adamson; 41(b) Sam Wong.

All art by Warren Clark.